The Table of the Lord

The Table of the Lord

Dominic Scotto, T.O.R.

SAINT BEDE'S PUBLICATIONS
Petersham, Massachusetts

St. Bede's Publications, Petersham, Massachusetts, 01366

97   96   95   94   93   92   91   90   5   4   3   2   1

LIBRARY OF CONGRESS CATALOGING-IN-PUBLICATION DATA

Scotto, Dominic F.
  Table of the Lord / Dominic F. Scotto.
      p.   cm.
  Includes bibliographical references.
  ISBN 0-932506-78-X
  1. Altars--History.   2. Catholic Church--Liturgy.   I. Title.
BV 195.S26   1990
247' .1--dc20
                                                      90-32824
                                                         CIP

Table of Contents

Introduction

Since the closing session of the Second Vatican Council multiple and significant liturgical changes have occurred within the Church, but it has been mentioned quite correctly that the two most visible changes brought into the life of the Church by the Council are the introduction of the vernacular into the liturgy and the mode of altar installation now apparent everywhere. However, it seems safe to assert that the new altar has since gained prevalence.

All of these changes concerning the altar have led us to a significant turning-point in the history of the equipping of the Christian Church because they have resulted in an abrupt change in a thousand-year-long trend which has seen the development, stage by stage, of increasingly elaborate altar superstructures. This development originated in the Carolingian Era when the altar became the resting place of expensively fashioned shrines containing the relics of the martyrs. Eventually, images of the martyrs and other religious scenes were added to the reliquaries. It is this practice which eventually helped lead to the development of the side altar. In the final stages of this trend, great masters were called upon to design and construct elaborate altar pieces with built-in tabernacles guarded by worshipping angels, all of which placed the crowning touch upon the massive structure which was the baroque altar.[1]

However, in churches built in today's new spirit, we generally see either of two layouts determined by the fact that a church is either a completely new structure or merely an old structure which has undergone adaptation.

In a completely new structure, the altar is usually just a simple table raised on a high podium, both fashioned of marble and well lighted from some hidden light source. On the other hand, if it is an older church with the traditional ostentatious baroque altar, this altar has been relegated to the background while a new altar, a relatively simple table free of all elaborate ornamentation, substitutes as the new focal point of all worship.[2]

We can ask ourselves the obvious question: what has caused these rather drastic changes? The answer to that question is that a radical reversal has occurred, a reemphasis of priorities from the peripheral, to the central, and the essential, all of which were the result of a long historical process once again returning to its origin.

In reality, however, it is not the purpose of the altar to serve as a visible revelation of the faith of the Church, nor is it meant to serve as an ostentatious exhibition of the wealth of the Church. Simply and practically, the altar is actually only a table, a table where the gifts of bread and wine are placed and transformed into the body and blood of Christ by the holy words uttered by the ministers of the Lord for the purpose of providing the people of God with the Bread of Life. It is a table around which the people of God gather and where the Church becomes visible as Church. This is exactly what happened at the Last Supper where the Apostles gathered around Christ the High Priest as he presided at the holy table. It was precisely here at this simple wooden table that a unique meal with a sacrificial background took place.[3]

However, is it possible for us to relive entirely that first simple beginning? In the intimacy of the upper room our Lord shared a meal with this small circle of his disciples, and it was at this same meal that the holy mystery was instituted. Thus in instituting this holy mystery Christ not only partook with his disciples of a paschal meal, but he gave this paschal meal its very own unique meaning.[4]

With the injunction to continue to do this as a memorial to him, the first followers of Christ continued to copy this image in its essential characteristics. However, in the very first century many considerable changes did occur. The congregations began to grow to such an extent that the intimacy of the small group service began to disappear. The entire meal service eventually fell by the wayside, and the prayer of thanksgiving and connected elements defined the essential character of the service. A distorted "meal form" is now all that remains of the original meal service.[5]

> But it is still a fact that after a thousand-year-long development the altar is essentially and rightfully what it was in the beginning: a table. It is no longer a distant exhibit, and the priest no longer stands on a distant platform. Priest and people have become one again.[6]

In view of these modern day developments, it is the purpose of this study to examine a particular period of this thousand-year-long development of the altar, namely the late Middle Ages, and to observe therein the development of Eucharistic theology and the popular piety expressed in devotion to the Blessed Sacrament. Having achieved this purpose, the final goal is then to demonstrate how these developments have been influential in producing a definite metamorphosis in the history of the altar as table of the Lord.

However, before we do so, I feel that it is first necessary to give a basic definition of the altar. Briefly we can say that essentially the altar is a table for sacrifice. We find that in the Old Testament the altar is looked upon as such a vital element of the entire sacrificial action that one could not conceive of a sacrifice without an altar upon which to offer the sacrifice. The object offered upon the altar as sacrifice became a victim not only by means of transformation or destruction but primarily through a ritualized cult performed by the priest offering the sacrifice. Therefore, the altar became not only the place upon which the sacrifice was offered but was seen more as a sacred symbol, the place where man encountered God. This encounter was not only vaguely hoped for but it was assured, because once the offering was religiously placed upon the altar, there was an assurance that God would willingly accept the sacrifice.[7]

The early Christian apologists, however, in fear of compromising the faith with Judaism and paganism, asserted that the concept of an altar which was valid for the ancient pagans and Jews did not apply to the Christian altar. Aristides maintained that God "does not require sacrifice and libation, nor even one of things visible; He requires not aught from any, but all living creatures stand in need of Him."[8] And Justin Martyr stated in like manner: "What sober-minded man, then, will not acknowledge that we are not atheists, worshipping as we do the Maker of this universe, and declaring, as we have been taught, that He has no need of streams of blood and libations and incense. . . . "[9] On the basis of this thinking, the Apologists explained that the Christians, therefore, had neither temple nor altar. The first Christians who "went as a body to the Temple every day but met in their houses for the breaking of bread . . . ,"[10] were keenly aware that the Church could not be localized in either Temple or home but that it was essentially a heavenly institution. For them the Christian altar was in heaven and so was the one true priest, Christ. Therefore, the highest sacrifice one would be able to offer him would be to acknowledge him as Lord and to render thanksgiving heavenward through songs of praise and hymns of glory.[11] According to Pseudo-Dionysius, the Christians of the sixth century certainly did have an altar, but it was the unique, incomparable altar which was Christ.[12]

Saint Paul affirms that the Christian altar is the"table of the Lord."[13] The altar is the table which bears the Lamb, the stone of sacrifice upon which Christ, through the ministry of his priest, prepares the wedding banquet, a feast which is the reenactment of his sacrifice effected for the deliverance and reconciliation of the faithful. The altar then becomes the focal point at which the meeting between God and his people is so wonderfully effected; it is at the altar that the *admirabile commercium*, the wonderful exchange, takes place between God and men.[14]

The primary function of the altar as the place upon which the sacrifice of Christ takes place is supplemented by its profound symbolic meaning.

> The stone has in effect a double biblical symbolism which makes it the image of Christ. First of all, the theme of the stone itself: the rock from which Moses made the water spring forth, "and that rock was Christ," (1 Cor. 10:4), a foundation rock or a rock from the corner of the edifice.
>
> Following the theme of the altar of stone, of which Genesis furnishes the first sketch (Gen. 28:18), and which is specified in the legislation of Deuteronomy for the offering of holocausts: in the New Law, Christ is the unique altar as he is the unique temple. From the Christ of which it is the image, the Christian altar carries as its stigmatas—five engraved crosses—and receives the ointment.[15]

Since the altar is anointed with holy chrism at its consecration, it is also seen as representative of Christ, the anointed one of the Holy Spirit.[16]

In these various interpretations of the altar, all seem to see the symbolism in the altar itself which derives its fundamental meaning and purpose from the sacred actions which are celebrated upon it. It is from the sacred liturgy, therefore, that the altar derives its profound dignity and holiness.

> From the liturgy, therefore and especially from the Eucharist, as from a fount, grace is poured forth upon us; and the sanctification of men in Christ and the glorification of God, to which all other activities of the Church are directed as towards their end, is achieved in the most efficacious possible way.[17]

Notes

[1] Josef Jungmann, "The New Altar," *Liturgical Arts*, XXXVII, (February, 1969), p. 36.

[2] *Ibid.*

[3] Cyril Pocknee, *The Christian Altar* (London: A.R. Mowbray and Company, Ltd., 1963), p. 33.

[4] G.T.H. Liesting, *The Sacrament of the Eucharist* (New York: Newman Press, 1968), p. 2.

[5] Josef Jungmann, *op. cit.*

[6] *Ibid.*

[7] Albert Gelin, "L'autel dans l'Ancien Testament," *La Maison-Dieu*, XXII (1952), pp. 9–17.

[8] Aristides, "Apology I," *The Ante-Nicene Fathers*, IX, ed. Allan Menzies (New York: Charles Scribners and Sons, 1903), p. 264.

[9] Justin, "The First Apology," *The Ante-Nicene Fathers*, I, ed. Alexander Roberts, James Donaldson, (New York: Charles Scribners and Sons, 1903), p. 166.

[10] Acts 2:46

[11] Josef Jungmann, *The Mass of the Roman Rite*, I, trans. Francis A. Brunner, (New York: Benzinger Brothers, Inc., 1951), pp. 24–25,

[12] Pseudo-Dionysius, "De Ecclesiastica hierarchia," *Patrologia Graeca*, ed. J. P. Minge. Vol. III (Paris, 1889), cols. 484–485.

[13] I Cor. 10:21.

[14] Jean Leclercq, "Le mystere de l'autel," *La Maison-Dieu*, XXIX (1952), pp. 60–70.

[15] *L'Eglise En Priere*, ed. A. G. Martimort, (Tournai: Desclee et Cie, 1961), p. 175.

[16] Oliver Rousseau, "Le Christ et l'autel: note sur la tradition patristique," *La Maison-Dieu*, XXIX (1952), pp. 32–39.

[17] "Constitution on the Sacred Liturgy," Art. 10. *Documents of Vatican II*, Walter M. Abbott, S.J., General Editor, (New York: The America Press, 1966).

Chapter I

The Altar—A Brief History

The traditional form of the Christian altar has been traced to the three distinct sources of table, tomb and altar. As table, the starting point of the Christian altar is the Holy Eucharist in the upper room on the first Maundy Thursday. It was here that a unique passover meal took place at a wooden table, a paschal meal to which the Lord Jesus gave a new and wonderful meaning. It seems that in imitation of the Lord, the first Christians continued to offer the sacrifice of the Mass in private homes, and to the celebration of the Eucharist they added a meal of fellowship.[1] It is not surprising then, that as devout Jews, they continued to speak of the altar as the Lord's table,[2] stressing the meal aspect of the Eucharist, an aspect with which they were thoroughly familiar. In these early Christian assemblies the same tables that were used for ordinary meals were in turn used to celebrate the Eucharist. Consequently, "the Christians were accused to atheism since they had no altars in the pagan or Jewish sense of objects set aside exclusively for sacrifice."[3] For over three centuries the altars continued to be made of wood.[4] These wooden altars did not rest permanently in these early church buildings. In one of his letters, Saint Cyprian spoke of a portable altar,[5] and the author of the *Quaestiones veteris et novi testimenti* mentioned that the deacons carried the altar into place at the beginning of the divine service and returned it to its normal place when the service had ended.[6]

Indeed the oldest picture of an altar which we possess in the cemetery of Saint Calixtus shows just such an altar: the priest is standing with outstretched arms near a tripod on which bread and a fish are placed. The very use of this table for the sacrifice helped to give it a special prestige as having been consecrated by the blood of Christ, and for a long time the consecration of an altar consisted in offering the sacrifice on it. No other rite was considered necessary.[7]

In general, the wooden tables pictured in the frescoes of the catacombs are of varied forms: some square, some round, and some semi-circular, some having three legs, but four legs being more common.[8] An early wooden altar is presently preserved in Saint John Lateran, Rome, while there is part of another altar preserved at Santa Pudentiana in the same city.

Saint Augustine also tells us about a wooden altar when he tells of an outrage committed by the Donatists against a Catholic bishop: "As he stood at the altar they beat him cruelly with clubs and such like weapons, and at last with broken pieces of timber from the altar itself."[9]

"The wooden altar, however, was soon replaced by one of stone."[10] Allegedly, the earliest decree requiring stone altars is one said to have been formulated by Pope Sylvester (314–335), to which there is a reference in the old Roman Breviary, Dedication of the Lateran, November 9, nocturn 2, lesson 6:

> The Blessed Sylvester afterwards decreed, when he was consecrating the altar of the Prince of the Apostles, that altars were thence-forward to be made of stone only, but not understanding this the Lateran Cathedral hath the altar made of wood.

But the authenticity of this decree is very questionable since it is most probably a forgery.[11]

It seems that it was actually Saint John Chrysostom (344–407), who first mentioned stone as the material for an altar.[12] Another early reference to stone altars is found in Saint Gregory of Nyssa (d. 394) when he says:

> This altar whereat we stand is by nature only common stone, nothing different from other stones, whereof our walls are made and our pavements adorned; but after it is consecrated and dedicated to the service of God, it becomes a holy table, an immaculate altar.[13]

Stone altars were first officially prescribed in 517,[14] by the French Synod of Epao, and eventually this particular legislation was incorporated into the Decree of Gratian which determined the practice of the universal Church.[15] Nonetheless, wooden altars remained in use in England as late as the eleventh century[16] and they continued in use through the ages up to the present time in the Ethiopian Church.[17] It was the Peace of Constantine (313 A.D.) which was responsible for this new development of the altar in its gradual movement from wood to stone, marble or precious metals. While the Church was still enduring persecutions, she was forced to be mobile, meeting and worshipping in secret. In order to allay the possibility of the profanation of the altar, it too had to be able to be easily and quickly moved in time of danger. However, once the Church had become legalized, it also became more fixed with designated church buildings and fixed altars. With the advent of fixed altars, it was but a short step from wood to stone as a material for the altar, since it was more dignified, more solid and much more in keeping with the stability of the Church.[18]

> Mystical considerations too influenced the idea that the altar should be of stone. Christ was Himself regarded as the altar of His own sacrifice; He was in His own words the Cornerstone upon which the holy temple of the faithful (the "living stones") should be built up. Naturally this symbolism was brought out more clearly by a stone altar.[19]

The custom of having stone altars soon became linked with the development of the cult of martyrs. The altar, symbolic of Christ, was seen as being incomplete without the members of Christ, and the martyrs were seen as the closest and most illustrious members, who had "washed their robes in the blood of the lamb,"[20] and are pictured as being "beneath the altar of God."[21] This mystical terminology was soon translated into actuality when the relics of the martyrs were placed in the altar itself.[22]

> The custom of burying relics in the altar does not derive from the alleged practice in times of persecution of celebrating the Holy Sacrifice directly on the martyrs' sarcophagi in the Catacombs. A more probable origin was the desire in the post-Constantine period, when churches in honor of the martyrs were being erected in large numbers, to bring the altar into as close contact as possible with the venerated tomb of the martyr, either by setting up the altar immediately above the tomb, which was below the floor of the church, or, when possible, by incorporating the sarcophagus in the altar itself.[23]

There were many different methods employed in order to achieve this particular effect, some of which were as follows: the relics were deposited in a depression in the top of the table or they were deposited in a precious box which in turn was placed inside the altar. An opening in front of the altar called a *cancellae* or *fenestella* allowed the faithful access to the relics both visually and physically. The faithful, in their deep devotion to the martyrs, customarily inserted cloths and other objects into the opening believing that by being brought into contact with the saint's tomb or sarcophagus these items acquired a healing value.[24]

In another more elaborate arrangement, the altar was placed directly above the tomb of the martyr which was located in a small room beneath the floor of the church. Access to the *confessio* or *martyrium* in which the body of the saint reposed was achieved by means of a staircase by the altar. According to Father Joseph Braun, this arrangement of the *martyrium* with its opening below the altar was one of the contributory causes for the celebrant having to stand on the other side of the altar facing the people, since there could be no foot-pace on the nave-side of the altar.[25] However, this assertion needs to be looked into more carefully.

In his great work, *Der christliche Altar in seiner geschichtlichen Entwicklung*, Father Joseph Braun, S.J. (1857–1947), proposed three basic reasons for the altar facing the people in the early church.

> First, in episcopal churches, where the cathedra of the bishop stood in the vertex of the apse behind the altar, it would have been too bothersome for the bishop and his ministers to go from the throne at the far end of the apse to the front side of the altar, as often as the sacred action would have demanded this. Second, when the altar was attached to a confessio (tomb of a saint), the celebrant assumed his place opposite the faithful to allow the latter to get as close as possible to the altar in order to venerate the relics buried beneath it and to lay pieces of cloth or other objects in the forechamber or confession of the tomb. Third, when the axis of the church was directed toward the west (northwest or southwest), the altar faced the nave so that the priest standing behind it could assume the customary meaningful direction toward the east.[26]

Let us now briefly examine these three assertions. First of all, a cursory examination of the early basilicas and the titular churches of Rome shows us that the principle of orientation had very little effect on the Latin liturgy, at least in Rome.[27] In fact, Leo I was strongly opposed to the practice of orientation as a remnant of paganism.[28] It was only in the Oriental and Gallican rites that the principle of orientation found general acceptance, although in later periods this concept did become strong in the West.[29] Fundamentally, it was an oriental practice to face the east while in prayer. The *Didascalia Apostolorum*, probably a North Syrian text of the early third century, indicates that the church building itself should be oriented to the east and that while at prayer all should face in that direction.

And in your congregations in the holy churches hold your assemblies with all decent order, and appoint the places for the brethren with care and gravity. And for the presbyters let there be assigned a place in the eastern part of the house; and let the bishop's throne be set in their midst, and let the presbyters sit with him. And again, let the lay men sit in another part of the house toward the east. For so it should be, that in the eastern part of the house the presbyters sit with the bishops, and next the lay men, and then the women; that when you stand up to pray, the rulers may stand first, and after them the lay men, and then the women also. For it is required that you pray toward the east, as knowing that which is written: "Give ye glory to God, who rideth upon the heaven of heavens toward the east."[30]

A similar directive is found in the Apostolic Constitution, also of Syrian provenance but of the late fourth century.[31] Franz Dolger (1879–1941), who according to Josef Jungmann wrote the best treatise on orientation,[32] maintained that except for Augustine and the Pseudo-Augustine no Western Father before the year 500 had given any indication that this particular oriental practice had influence in the West.[33] However, Paulinus of Nola (d. 431), did affirm the existence of oriented churches in the West.[34]

The *Ordo Romanus Primus* seems to be the only Roman document which speaks of orientation at Mass. In part it speaks of the Roman Pontiff kissing the book of the gospels and the altar and then retiring to his seat. The particular text which most concerns us however, is the following:

When they have finished, the pontiff turns toward the people and begins the Gloria in excelsis Deo. And immediately he turns to the East until it is finished. After this he turns again to the people and says: Pax Vobis, and turning to the East he says: Oremus, and the oration follows.[35]

In commenting on this text, Michel Andrieu (1886–1956) asserted that this particular rubric seems to be most certainly a Gallic addition to the original Roman Ordo.[36]

With this testimony it seems, therefore, that celebrating Mass with one's back to the people could also have originated in Gaul. The construction of oriented churches having the apse facing east and the facade facing west would have necessitated this practice since the celebrant would normally have assumed a position facing the apse and therefore would have his back to the people.[37]

As a result of this brief look into the practice of orientation, it seems most unlikely, therefore, that in the West this principle had anything to do with the custom of facing the people when offering the Mass. Rather it seems to be the most likely cause for the discontinuance of this practice.[38]

With the contemporary emphasis placed on the position of the altar as a prime pastoral factor for effecting a union of minds and hearts of both celebrant and congregation, it would be well to keep in mind that any historical precedent for such a practice in the early church is very often an exaggeration. In our own day and age the various Oriental rites continue to celebrate the liturgy with the minister's back to the people, and it is well to note that these rites have been generally more faithful in preserving the primitive, traditional practices of the Church since they have always retained the people's active participation in the liturgy. According to Father Josef Jungmann, "the principal reason for the existence of such a custom in the position of the altar can be traced to the general rule of orientation in prayer."[39]

In Rome it was common for churches to be oriented in such a fashion that the facade faced the east while the apse faced the west. Roman temples were originally thus oriented in deference to Sol, the sun god, in order that the rays of the rising sun would fall upon the idol whenever the doors of the temple would be opened. Roman public buildings followed this same architectural trend; but now for completely different reasons, the oldest Christian churches too, at least in Rome, were built in this fashion. This was done not in honor of Sol, the sun god, but in deference to Christ our sun, the sun of justice and the Son of God, who would come again like the rising sun from the east. Therefore, in Rome, with the churches oriented in this way, the celebrant would have to have his back to the apse which was oriented to the west in order to face the east and the people. In prayer the people also would face the east and thus would have their backs to the priest as he stood in prayer.[40]

According to Jungmann, it seems that since the disposition of the altar in the Roman basilicas of the period allowed the priest to face the altar and the east simultaneously, it is likely that this practice is connected with this orientation in prayer. For the faithful, however, to have to turn from the celebrant and the altar in order to face the east seemed to be a decided disadvantage, even though they turned around only during periods of prayer. For example, we have preserved for us in the Egyptian liturgies "a command, in Greek, by which the faithful are told to turn to the east at least during the main prayer of the liturgy, before the Sanctus of the Mass."[41]

> But it was most probably this inconvenience which finally led to a change in planning the church building. As early as the fourth century, some churches were built with the apse towards the east, in accordance with what became the general custom later on. Now the priest is standing at the altar, generally built of stone, as the leader of his people; the people look up to him and at the altar at the same time, and together with the priest they face towards the east. Now the whole congregation is like a huge procession, being led by the priest and moving east towards the sun, towards Christ the Lord.[42]

The second reason given by Braun for the altar facing the people is that it was attached to a *confessio* (the tomb of a saint). Obviously, in our previous development of the *confessio*, we can see how this would have prevented the priest from standing on the side of the altar nearer the people. However, the altar facing the people is a practice that ante-dated the construction of a *confessio* under altars. According to Felice Grossi-Grandi, the *confessio* found in Saint Paul's Basilica in Rome was the first example of this type, and it dated only from the sixteenth century.[43]

Although the *confessio* did exist before this period, it took the form of a crypt behind or beneath the altar rather than a deep pit located in front of the altar. Even in its earlier form, however, the *confessio* dates only from the period of the transfer of martyrs' relics from the catacombs to the Roman churches, namely from the sixth century.[44] At least two centuries before this, the altar *versus populum* seems to have existed in those oldest Christian churches which were constructed during the reign of the Emperor Constantine.[45] It is also relevant to this point that contemporary researches and explorations of Saint Peter's in Rome have established with fair certitude that originally the reputed shrine or *martyrium* of Saint Peter was not directly connected with the altar but was situated apart from it and that it was located completely above the floor level of the church. It was only in the sixth century, most probably during the reign of Pope Pelagius II (579–590), that the altar became directly associated with the shrine. This happened:

> when the floor of the sanctuary was raised up so that part of the martyrium was sunk below floor level; and the altar thus became associated with the shrine by being built over the confessio. The siting of the altar

in relation to the martyrium before this sixth century innovation is, at best, uncertain.[46]

It does not seem very likely, therefore, that the veneration of the martyrs was the motivating factor in constructing the altar *versus populum*.

It seems, then, that the most significant factor in the practice of offering Mass while facing the people rests in the very first assertion made by Braun, namely the location of the bishop's throne. While the altar was certainly dominant, the bishop's throne occupied the central position in the church, that is, at the very apex of the apse.[47] In moving to the altar from the throne it was most natural and convenient for the bishop to go directly to the side of the altar nearest to him.[48] While convenience was undoubtedly a significant cause, it seems that there were many other factors which may have influenced the development of this practice. Presently, however, in light of all the available research, it seems that there exists no conclusive evidence to support the theory that the motive for offering Mass *versus populum* was a purely theological one.[49]

As the cult of the martyrs grew in the post-Constantinian period, more and more churches were built which were in truth burial churches, that is churches which housed the sarcophagus of some martyr. This increased veneration of martyrs soon created a demand that this cult be expressed in other churches as well. But since it was unthinkable to venerate the martyrs away from their actual tombs, "notional" burial churches were built to meet the people's demands, churches in which relics of the saints were either buried under or within the altar. In the first of these churches the relics were merely pieces of cloth which had been touched to the *martyrium* or directly to the relics themselves through the opening in front of the *martyrium*. From the ninth century on, however, the bodies of the martyrs themselves began to be partitioned so that in the west these "notional churches" now had genuine relics of their own.

Another influential factor which led to the transference of the relics to urban churches was the fear of desecration and loss because of the Germanic invasions. "By the seventh century it was the rule that every church should be dedicated to a saint, and an integral part of the Roman altar consecration was the burial of relics."[50]

The portioning of the bodies of saints eventually led to the seventh-eighth century custom of enclosing these relics in the top of the altar-slab either in a shallow cavity or in a deeper opening known as the *sepulcrum* or sepulchre.[51] Along with the insertion of the bones of saints, there were included three grains of incense signifying burial spices, along with three fragments of a consecrated host.[52]

There is evidence that as early as the year 500 in certain places it was customary during the rite of consecration for the bishop to anoint the altar top with the oil of holy chrism in the middle and at the four corners with the sign of the cross.[53] Since the mensa had been previously washed with holy water the striking connection between the consecration of the altar and the rite of baptism-confirmation was underscored.

In the twenty-sixth canon of the Council of Epao (517), this type of anointing was forbidden if the altar was not made of stone.[54] However, since the origin of this particular rite of the consecration of an altar was Gallican, it was not until the eighth or ninth century that it became adopted at Rome.[55]

Despite the insistence of the Council of Epao and succeeding councils as well that only stone altars were to be consecrated, circumstances did make it necessary at times for Mass to be celebrated on a wooden table. Missionaries traveling in countries where there were no churches, armies moving on campaigns, such as the Crusaders, on board ship and other such occasions dictated the use of wooden tables instead of stone altars. Also the homes and castles of important people usually contained an oratory at which there were times when Mass had to be celebrated. To be able to adjust to these various situations a "super-altar" was devised. This "super-altar" consisted of a small rectangle or square of stone, consecrated by a bishop, which could then be carried around by a priest. When Mass was to be celebrated this square of stone could be inserted into the sepulcrum of an unconsecrated table or altar, or it was simply placed in the middle of a table and the Eucharistic action would take place over it with the chalice and paten standing upon it.[56]

In the fourth century we first encounter evidence for the erection of a baldachin or *ciborium* over the altar, a canopy-like structure resting on four columns covering both the altar and its foot-pace.[57] It was usually made of stone, marble, wood or metal. The wooden structures were usually sheathed with metal. The most usual material, however, was stone or marble, although the canopy which was presented by Constantine the Great (d. 337) to the Lateran Basilica was of silver, since it is described in the *Liber Pontificalis* as *fastidium argenteum battutilem*.[58] There is a great difference of opinion among authors concerning the origin of the baldachin. While Edmund Bishop (1871–1917) interpreted the baldachin as an example of the ancient tendency to veil sacred objects,[59] and Noele Boulet gave his support to this particular opinion,[60] Eisenhofer and Lechner suggest that perhaps the custom could have been derived from the Byzantine court where the canopy over the emperor's throne was called the ciborium.[61] They also, however, refer to the opinion of Heisenberg (1869–1930), who put forth the theory that the canopy was an element taken directly from Phoenician religious thought and Syro-Hellenic art, which in turn influenced the building of the structure over the site of the tomb of Christ located in the Church of the Resurrection in Jerusalem.[62] As a matter of fact, the term *ciborium* is directly derived from the Semitic word for tomb.[63] Peter Anson shows preference for the opinion that the *ciborium* does indeed come from the Byzantine court arrangement, since it bears such a close resemblance to the *tegurium* which extended over the seat of the chief magistrate in the civil basilicas and which also extended over the statues of Roman deities.[64] Since, however, the word *tegurium* is just a corruption of the word *ciborium*, there really seems to be very little difference in these views.[65]

There are no complete *ciboria* which have been preserved from the earlier centuries of the Church. Of those *ciboria* which have been preserved from a later period the most notable are to be found in the churches of central and northern Italy. The earliest one remaining in its original position dates from the year 812 and is located in the church of Saint Appolinare in Classe, Ravenna.[66]

From the fourteenth century onwards, the *ciborium* had been adapted to meet the changed conditions where the altar came to be placed close to an altar screen or an east wall with a large window. It was rare to find a window in the space of a Roman basilica, and the free-standing altar usually stood on the chord of the apse. In Northern Europe, however, where daylight was a consideration because of a very lack of it, the large and low east window was developed. In these particular conditions the ciborium standing on its heavy columns proved to be an obstruction and so had to undergo adaptation. While the posts were retained around the altar, they now were fashioned in a much more slender form as ridel posts supporting curtains but not the canopy itself. Meanwhile, in order to permit a maximum of natural light to enter the church, the canopy proper was raised above the window and suspended from the roof, and in this form it became known as a *tester*. The canopy or tester retained its usual square shape and continued to cover both the foot-pace and the altar. The tester was gradually made of wood and gilded and decorated, but in Rome and central Italy the primitive use of the marble *ciborium* was never abandoned.[67]

The custom of veiling an altar in the west had been another subject which has caused many differences of opinions among scholars, differences which still remained basically unresolved. During the seventh and eighth centuries at Rome, the *Liber Pontificalis* provides us with some more definite evidence on this subject. It leaves no doubt that during this period veils or curtains were indeed suspended all around the *ciboria* of the great Roman basilicas. That the altar also had veils on all four sides of the *ciborium* seems quite certain for Pope Sergius (795–816), gave to Saint Peter's eight veils, four of white and four of scarlet,[68] and Pope John VI (701–705), gave a set of altar veils to the Church of Saint Paul outside-the-walls.[69] Pope Leo III (795–816), also gave several sets of veils to the Lateran Basilica and Saint Paul's outside-the-walls, which were in various colors and which were occasionally decorated with precious stones.[70] The use of the term *tetravela* in these examples given to us in the *Liber Pontificalis* implies definite Greek influence. It is well known that during the seventh and eighth centuries there was a considerable colony of Greeks and Syrians at Rome; moreover, several Popes of that period are known to have been of Greek or Syrian origin. Since the veiling of the altar was a custom practiced in the East, it could very well be, therefore, that this practice was introduced at Rome through their influence. As to exactly when the veils were drawn during this period, the *ordines Romani* offers us no evidence.[71] Presently, the rods for holding the veils may still be seen on all four sides of a number of italian *ciboria* as well as in illustrations contained in many old manuscripts. In more than one of the Anglo-Saxon Pontificals belonging to the late tenth century there is attestation to the fact that the curtain or veil was drawn before the altar in connection with the rite of consecration of the altar by the bishop. There is also evidence that the sanctuary was veiled at the consecration of the altar during the ninth and tenth centuries in France.[72]

The ninth-century Carolingian era was a time of great transition in the life of Western Christendom. Many innovations were introduced which eventually were going to exert great influence upon matters affecting the administration of the sacraments. References to some of the ceremonial changes of that period may be found in the writings of Alcuin (d. 804), Amalarius of Metz (d. circa 850) and Rabanus Maurus (d. 856). However, for a particular innovation that was going to have a marked effect upon the structure and development of the altar we turn to a Synodical Admonition, attributed to Pope Leo IV (847–855), but most likely of Gallican origin and incorporated into many tenth century documents. In part it reads:

> Let nothing be placed upon the altar except the chests and relics, or perhaps the four gospels and a pyx, with the body of the Lord for the viaticum of the sick.[73]

Up to this time, the only objects permitted to be placed on the altar were the *oblata*, the sacred vessels for the Eucharist and the Book of the Gospels. The placing of anything else, such as cross or candlesticks, upon the altar during this earlier period had been discouraged and forbidden. Therefore, this new permissive attitude which allowed for the placing of chests with relics on the *mensa* was in effect a violation of a hitherto carefully observed principle.[74]

The cult of the martyrs was a movement which saw its first development in the second century. Nevertheless, it was in the ninth century that popular devotion to the relics of the saints became widespread.

> It was in this century that many relics were enshrined for the first time and "elevated" (placed over altars for public veneration). Up to this time the high altar stood out in church as the prominent feature, the table, the stone of sacrifice, being kept unencumbered and treated with special respect. Now it began to be invaded by reliquaries, placed either on the table, or, the larger ones, enshrined behind and above the altar. This relic invasion was destined to change, little by little, the character, disposition and even the situation of the high altar.[75]

Generally, relics were classified as either the entire body of a saint or a portion of that body, some article of clothing worn by him or pieces of cloth which had been touched to his body or tomb. To these relics we may add relics or fragments of the True Cross. Many of these relics were contained in small caskets which were placed on the altar during Mass. Sometimes these small reliquaries became incorporated into a small portable triptych which was placed on the back portion of the altar.[76]

As we have already noted, in the earlier period of the Western Church, the complete bodies of saints were buried under the altar since there was an aversion to the dismemberment and translation of the body. The sixth century, however, first witnessed the dismemberment of the bodies of saints as an increasingly acceptable custom. The portions of the venerable remains were incorporated or carried in portable reliquaries and shrines of various forms.[77]

In the great churches, however, which were fortunate enough to possess the body of a famous saint, it was considered as essential not to dismember that body but to place it in some rich coffer or reliquary since this would inevitably bring large numbers of pilgrims to the church. With the growth of the number of pilgrims visiting these shrines, there developed a similar growth in the demand that these reliquaries be given greater prominence and displayed to greater advantage. Since the reliquary or shrine had previously been locked under the altar, some compromise had to be reached which would be able to combine the altar with the increased prominence to be given the reliquary. The question was eventually settled by placing the smaller reliquaries directly on the altar and by enshrining the larger ones behind and above the altar with one end of the shrine resting directly on a small back portion of the altar and the other end extending directly beyond the altar and supported by stone or marble pillars or masonry. The shrine thus began to act as a retable to the altar.[78]

The ever-growing relic shrine led to a change in the altar. The smallish, square design yielded to a much larger altar in oblong form. It also led in time to the abandonment of the *confessio* and to the gradual disappearance of the civory. Furthermore, the civory came to be transferred from a position immediately over the altar to one over the shrine.[79]

In the approximate time zone of the eleventh century, this led to the eventual placement of the lights on the altar—at first only during Mass. The lights had previously been suspended from the roof of the civory. The cross, which had heretofore hung from the canopy or surmounted it or had simply stood on the floor in the vicinity of the altar, also came to rest on the altar. Hence, the reliquary, having slowly but surely become ever bigger and ever more ornate, had eventually come to dominate as the center of attraction, the altar assuming a supportive role.

All these changes in the altar, in the second period of its history, came about not by the legislation of the Church, but through the increasing pressure of popular piety, ever exalting the accessory at the expense of the principal.[80]

With the increased crowds of pilgrims arriving at any celebrated shrine, it became necessary to move the shrine further east for reasons of accessibility. This achieved the final separation of the altar from its shrine by the end of the fourteenth and the beginning of the fifteenth century. At this time a stone screen was erected behind the high altar of a number of the greater churches with the shrine being placed east of the screen. This arrangement allowed the pilgrims to pray at the shrine without interrupting the services held in the choir and at the altar.[81]

Toward the end of the fourteenth century, the retables, originally low in height and of a temporary nature, began to develop into higher and more permanent structures. They gradually grew bigger and more complex and ornate in design, some of them even divided into storeys. These enormous reredoses sometimes used the altar itself as a foundation and sometimes were self-supportive behind the altar, but they always seemed to give the impression that the altar was nothing other than a "serviceable base for a super-incumbent mass of ornamentation."[82]

As a result of this entire development, the high altars of this period were characteristically large and overly ornamented, features which were very much in keeping with the spirit of the Renaissance, with Baroque and Rococo styles of architecture, and with the popular piety of the period.

> The result of this mania for immense, elaborate super-structures was that the altar itself, the table of sacrifice, lost all its significance, was dwarfed out of all recognition and ceased to be the focal point of the church.[83]

Notes

[1] Acts 2:46; Josef Jungmann, *The Mass of the Roman Rite*, I, trans. Francis A. Brunner, (New York: Benziger Brothers, Inc., 1951), pp. 7–22.

[2] 1 Cor. 10–21.

[3] William J. O'Shea, *The Worship of the Church* (Maryland: The Newman Press, 1958), p. 166; Jungmann, *op. cit.*, pp. 24–25.

[4] R.X. Redmond, "Altar—Historical Development," *The New Catholic Encyclopedia*, Vol. I, (McGraw-Hill Book Company, New York, 1967), p. 347.

[5] Cyprian, "Epistola XLV," *Corpus scriptorum ecclesiasticorum latinorum*, ed. William Hartel, Vol. III, Pars II (Vienna, 1871), pp. 600–601.

[6] "Quaestiones Veteris et Novi Testamenti," *Patrologia Latina*, ed. J. P. Migne, Vol. XXXV (Paris, 1841), col. 2301.

[7] O'Shea, *op. cit.*

[8] Henri Leclercq, "Autel," *Dictionnaire d'archeologie chretienne et de liturgie*, Vol. I, Pars. II (Paris, 1924), cols. 3158–3161.

[9] Augustine, "Epistola CLXXXV—Ad Bonifacium," *Patrologia Latina*, ed. J. P. Migne, Vol. XXXIII (Paris, 1841), col. 803.

[10] F. van der Meer and Christine Mohrmann, *Atlas of the Early Christian World*, trans. and ed. Mary F. Hedlund and H. H. Rowley, (London: Thomas Nelson and Sons Ltd., 1958), p. 139.

[11] Leclercq, *op. cit.*, 3168.

[12] Chrysostom, "Homilia in Epistolam secunda ad Corinthios," XX, *Patrologia Graeca*, ed. J. P. Migne. Vol. X (Paris, 1862), cols. 539–540.

[13] Gregory of Nyssa, "In Baptismum Christi," *Patrologia Graeca*, ed. J. D. Minge. Vol. XLVI (Paris, 1863), col. 581.

[14] *Sacrorum Conciliorum Nova et Amplissima Collectio*, ed. J.D. Mansi, Vol. VIII, Can. XXVI (Florence, 1762), col. 562.

[15] Decretum Gratiani, Pars. III, Causa XXXI, Distinctiones I: "De Consecratione," cited in Ludwig Eisenhofer Joseph Lechner, *The Liturgy of the Roman Rite*, trans. A. J., and E. F. Peeler, ed. H. E. Winstone, (New York: Herder and Herder, 1961), p. 121

[16] Geoffrey Webb, *The Liturgical Altar*, (London: Washbourne and Bogan, Ltd., 1933), p. 26.

[17] Archdale A. King, *Rites of Eastern Christendom*, I, (Rome: Tipographia Poliglotta Vaticana, 1947), pp. 553–554.

[18] William O'Shea, *The Worship of the Church*, (Maryland: The Newman Press, 1958), p. 167.

[19] *Ibid*.

[20] Rev. 7:14.

[21] Rev. 6:9.

[22] O'Shea, *op. cit.*, pp. 167–168.

[23] Eisenhofer, Lechner, *op. cit.*

[24] Joseph Braum, *Der christliche Altar in seiner geistlichen Entwicklung* (Munich: Koch and Company, 1924), I, pp. 412–413.

[25] *Ibid.*

[26] *Ibid.*

[27] Henri Leclercq, "Orientation," *Dictionnaire d'archeologie chretienne et de liturgie*, Vol. XII, Pars II (Paris, 1936), cols. 2665–2666.

[28] Franz J. Dolger, *Sol Salutis* (Munster, 1925), pp. 3–5.

[29] Johannes Quasten, *Monumenta eucharistica et liturgica vetustissima, Florilegium Patristicum*, VII, (Bonn: Peter Hanstein, 1935), p. 35.

[30] *Didascalia Apostolorum*, ed. R. Hugh Connolly, (Oxford: The Clarendon Press, 1929), pp. 119–120.

[31] *Didascalia et Constitutiones Apostolorum*, ed. F. X. Funk, (Paderborn: Libraria Ferdinandi Schoening, 1905), II, 57, pp.2–5.

[32] Josef Jungmann, *The Early Liturgy* (Notre Dame: University of Notre Dame Press, 1959), p. 134.

[33] Dolger, *op. cit.*, p. 255

[34] Paulinus of Nola, "Epistola XXXII," *Patrologia Latina*, ed. J. P. Migne. Vol. LXI (Paris, 1847), col. 337.

[35] Michel Andrieu, *Les Ordines Romani du Haut Moyen Age*, II, (Louvain: Spicilegium Sacrum Lovanense, 1948), pp. 83–84.

[36] Michel Andrieu, "Note sur une ancienne redaction de l'Ordo Romanus Primus," *Revue des Sciences Religieuses*, I, (1921), pp. 394–395.

[37] Leclercq, "Orientation," *op. cit.*

[38] John H. Miller, "Altar Facing the People, Fact or Fable?" *Worship*, XXXIII, (January, 1959), pp. 85–86.

[39] Jungmann, *The Early Liturgy*, p. 138.

[40] *Ibid.*, pp. 136–138.

[41] *Ibid.*

[42] *Ibid.*

[43] Felice Grossi-Gondi, *I Monumenti Cristiani* (Roma: Universita Gregoriana, 1923), p. 431.

[44] *Ibid.*, p. 429.

[45] Jungmann, *The Early Liturgy*, p. 137.

[46] Cyril Pocknee, *The Christian Altar* (London: A. R. Mowbray and Company, Ltd., 1963), p. 38.

[47] Braun, *op. cit.*

[48] *Ibid.*

[49] Miller, *op. cit.*, pp. 88–89.

[50] *The Gelasian Sacramentary*, ed. H. A. Wilson (Oxford: 1894), p. 133. Cited in Eisenhofer, Lechner, *op. cit.*, pp. 121–122.

[51] Braun, *op. cit.*, pp. 656 ff.

[52] Andrieu, *Les Ordines Romani*, IV, pp. 389–400.

[53] *Ibid*, pp. 324–325.

[54] Mansi, *op. cit.*

[55] Andrieu, *op. cit.*, p. 385.

[56] Braun, *op. cit.*, pp. 444–517.

[57] Noele-Maurice Boulet, "L'autel dans l'antiquité chretienne," *La Maison-Dieu*, XXIX (1952), p. 45.

[58] L. Duchesne, *Le Liber Pontificalis* (Paris: E. De Boccard, 1955), I, p. 172.

[59] E. Bishop, *Liturgica Historica* (Oxford: The Clarendon Press, 1918), p. 22.

[60] Boulet, *op. cit.*, pp. 22–23.

[61] Eisenhofer, Lechner, *op. cit.*, p. 123.

[62] A. Heisenberg, *Brabeskirche und Apostelkirche*, I (Leipzig, 1908), pp. 215–216, cited by Eisenhofer-Lechner, *Ibid.*

[63] Braun, *op. cit.*, II, p. 190.

[64] Peter Anson, *Churches: Their Plan and Furnishing* (Milwaukee: The Bruce Publishing Company, 1948), p. 100.

[65] John H. Miller, *Fundamentals of the Liturgy* (Notre Dame: Fides Publishers, Inc., 1962), p. 100.

[66] van der Meer, Mohrmann, *op. cit.*, pp. 96–97.

[67] Webb, *op. cit.*, pp. 28–30.

[68] Duchesne, *op. cit.*, p. 373.

[69] *Ibid.*, p. 383.

[70] *Ibid.*, II, p. 29.

[71] Andrieu, *op. cit.*, II.

[72] L. Duchesne, *Christian Worship* (London: S.P.C.K., 1904), p. 413.

[73] Pope Leo IV, "Admonitio Synodalis Antiqua," *Patrologia Latina*, ed. J. P. Migne, Vol. CXXXII (Paris, 1853), col. 456.

[74] Pocknee, *op. cit.*, p. 84.

[75] J.B. O'Connell, *Church Building and Furnishing* (Notre Dame: University of Notre Dame Press, 1955), pp. 134–135.

[76] Pocknee, *op. cit.*

[77] *Ibid.*

[78] *Ibid.*, pp. 84–85.

[79] Bishop, *op. cit.*, p. 27.

[80] O'Connell, *op. cit.*

[81] Webb, *op. cit.*

[82] Bishop, *op. cit.*, p. 30.

[83] O'Connell, *op. cit.*, p. 136.

Chapter II

Themes of Eucharistic, Popular Piety in the Middle Ages

The early Christians celebrated a form of liturgy which was essentially corporate and public. The altar is closely connected with the worshipping community and the sacrificial meal which is celebrated is clearly seen as the consummate goal of the celebration, facts which are amply proved to us by liturgical forms which have endured through the centuries to this day. The Carolingian Age, however, with its uniformly rich, liturgical literature demonstrates how the clergy now consciously detaches itself from the body of the faithful during the heart of the Eucharistic liturgy and retreats deep into the sanctuary while the congregation can only follow from a distance the outward, visible action of the celebration. The altar now becomes withdrawn from the people and private Masses begin to be celebrated causing an eventual proliferation of side altars in the church. During the celebration of Mass the celebrant now has his back to the people and the spiritual action in the Canon is in its isolation essentially hidden from the assembly. This tendency will be later transformed into a silent Canon which was forbidden to be translated into the vernacular. "To all intents and purposes the faithful had become merely spectators at the sacrifice."[1]

What are the factors that caused this contrast to develop? These factors are many and diverse, but the changes are so gradual and difficult to pin down precisely, that at best we can merely outline some of the main themes of change in Eucharistic, popular piety and the general conditions which helped to elicit these changes.

Our first consideration will be the national factors which forged the religious-cultural stamp of the early Middle Ages. In this initial approach we cannot overlook the cultural heritage of the Greek Orient which greatly influenced the West, principally the Gallo-

Frankish part of Europe.[2] However, since there is such a marked difference in the final forms of the liturgy in East and West, the influence was not one of simple transference or of pure reproduction. The representation of Christ in the East as Pantocrator certainly does not coincide with the West's concept of Christ in his historical and human epiphany terminating in the all-dominant figure of the Crucified. Eastern piety also possessed a much stronger and excessively eschatological bent than that of the West, a tendency which even exceeded that of primitive Christianity and which was characterized by a continuous and total expectation of Resurrection and final glorification.[3]

However, despite the differences there are many decisive points which illustrate a definite experience shared by East and West alike. The decline in importance of the Trinity and of the role of Christ as mediator was a phenomenon that occurred both in East and West as was the phenomenon of the growth of the cult of Mary. It is decisive points such as these which cause us to view Arianism and the consequent reaction against it as one of the chief factors influencing the spiritual and liturgical development of both East and West.[4]

The essence of Arianism is rooted in the principle that the Son of God is less than the Father and was created by the Father out of nothingness. Consequently, Jesus Christ cannot be truly God because he is subordinated to the Father who can have no equal. "It attacked, in fact, the very nature of Christianity, because it attributed redemption to a God who was not a true God at all and for this reason incapable of redeeming mankind. Thus, it deprived the faith of its essential character."[5]

This belief is a result of a theological rationalism which gained much support simply because it was able to give a simple and easy answer to a very difficult theological question, namely, the type of relationship which existed between God the Father and God the Son.[6] The controversy which ensued over Arianism had the effect of producing in the West an exaggerated emphasis of the divinity of Christ which in turn had the effect of overshadowing his role as mediator and high priest. This entire movement continued to influence the development of medieval piety.[7]

This overstress on the divinity of Christ unavoidably led to the coalescence of the notion of God and Christ which made the mediation of Christ as God-man all the more difficult to understand. As a result of this polemic even the wording of liturgical prayers was affected. Prayers such as doxologies, which formerly emphasized the humanity and mediatorship of Christ, now were changed to emphasize the divinity of Christ and his oneness in nature with God.[8] However, this shift of emphasis was not the result of polemics alone but of the general religious climate of the time as well. This same climate was correspondingly favorable to the development of a relatively new religious phenomenon, namely, the veneration of the saints. Deprived of the mediatorship of Christ, the people now turned with great fervor to a multitude of saints, advocates who from exalted positions as "friends of God," might be called upon to act as intermediaries between man and the otherwise unapproachable majesty of God."[9]

Among other things, church furnishings soon began to be influenced by this new phenomenon. The image of Christ continued to dominate, and in the form of the crucifix it was usually set high on the triumphal arch or some comparable place. Eventually the crucifix is located on the altar between candles. "As the central ornament of the altar it began to come into general use in the fifteenth century although it had occasionally been so used earlier."[10] Nevertheless, the altar-pieces which were beginning to grow and multiply in the late Carolingian period, were always dominated by the figure of a saint, usually the sainted martyr whose relics reposed in the altar. During this same period the table form of the altar was gradually changing into a rectangular block form which was more conducive to the interment of relics.[11]

Men relentlessly hunted for relics of martyrs with extraordinary zeal and built thousands of shrines to house them in an effort to win the favor and intercession of these saints. A movement such as this would not have been so extensive in scope had it not been for the fact that Christ as Redeemer had all but lost his mediatorial and human aspects and was now being adored as one with the Father in awesome divinity. A vacuum had been created and devotion to the saints filled this vacuum in the lives of the faithful.[12]

Despite this development, our Lord's earthly form did not entirely disappear from the scene but took on the aspect of being simply the epiphany of God. Maintaining traditional Church teaching, especially about the two natures of Christ, the Savior's earthly appearance was viewed as but the point of God's operation. All human will and feeling in Christ receded as he took on the aspect of a Teutonic hero-ideal, the all-powerful King of Heaven with infinite

might. The humanity of Christ is all but obliterated by his divinity
and despite his human actions and sufferings the names "God" and
"Creator" are continually applied to him. This type of language is
prevalent in the late Middle Ages, and it is only after the Council of
Trent, when preachers were required to be more thoroughly trained
in theology, that it gradually declines.

> We must, therefore, call to mind that as well as the shift of accent
> brought about by the reaction to Arianism at the beginning of the Middle
> Ages, we must also take into account the tendency to simplification and
> coarsening of the gospel message, a process which took place most of all
> where contact with the sources of the Faith had grown weak and where
> intellectual analysis of the substance of Faith was neglected.[13]

The effects of these developments also influenced Christian art of
the High Middle Ages. Where previously God the Father was portrayed symbolically, now, due in great measure to the lack of distinction between God and Christ, He is depicted in human form.
Christ is generally portrayed in splendor, usually a gigantic and
potent figure in the majestic garb of Cosmocrator, the victorious
Christ-God.[14]

Obviously, Christian piety must always essentially revolve about
the person of Christ. If the religious thought of the early Middle
Ages tended to merge the glory of Christ with that of the Trinity,
then devotion to Christ had to find other modes of expression.
While the Byzantine Orient stressed the deification of the humanity
of Christ, the West stressed the fundamental mysteries of the work
of salvation, the Incarnation and the death on the Cross which now
became springboards for further development.[15]

In due time the controversy over the person of Christ moved
inexorably to the mystery of the Incarnation and the Virgin birth.
By the fourth century Mariology became the center of contention
between Arian and Catholic teachers. With the additional threat of
Nestorianism and its belief that Mary gave birth to a purely human
being, Marian dogma had to be staunchly defended. The Church
now begins to refer to Mary as Theotokos, the Mother of God, a title
which was officially attributed to her at the Council of Ephesus in
431. Churches began to be dedicated to Mary, and the rise of Marian feast days gave the newly assured dogmas the proper mode of
expression. From the East, where they originated, these Marian feast
days moved to the West where by the seventh century they became

included in the official calendar of the Church of the West.[16] Popular devotion to Mary simply sought her mediation with God which was in reality nothing else but a substitute for the mediatorship of Christ, a pivotal dogmatic fact no longer clearly understood by the faithful. Therefore, it was inevitable that wherever Christological heresies were more deeply rooted in the West, there veneration to Mary was most pronounced.[17]

Gradually, the poetry, art and popular devotion of the Middle Ages became strongly affected by the Marian theme, which nevertheless does not appear in isolation but remains involved with and subservient to the mystery of the Incarnation. In the later Middle Ages, the Marian theme is seen to become more and more allied with the entire story of the childhood and youth of the Savior. The Creed and the liturgical year help to remind the faithful of the centrality and dominance of Christ in his personhood and in those events of his life connected with the great events of salvation. Thus, an entirely new religious piety began to develop in the late Middle Ages.

> This new piety, characterized by its orientation to the concrete, its vehemence and the immediacy of expression, and its strongly personal nature, transferred its attention from the living actuality of the glorified Christ to the earthly, suffering and dying Savior.[18]

Eventually this led to a conception of the Mass as a mere memorial of Christ's passion, a memorial totally exclusive of any consideration of his Resurrection and final glory. "All this is nothing but the final development of the medieval overemphasis on the suffering humanity of Christ."[19]

The reason for this evolution of medieval devotion to Christ cannot be explained as the direct result of the Church's reaction to Teutonic Arianism since the evolution was quite different in the East. Despite racial and moral differences, which were quite significant, the single most important factor was the West's unique approach to anti-Arian Christology. Following the Council of Chalcedon in 451 which made a clear distinction between the two natures of Christ, the eventual tendency in the West was to overstress the divine nature in Christ to such a degree that the role of his human nature for redemption was overlooked. This is precisely the type of approach the West adopted in the fight against Arianism.[20]

With these currents of change affecting basic Catholic thought, it was only a matter of time before other spheres of faith were affected as well. The conception of Church and sacraments were two such areas most notably affected. With the heavy underscoring of Christ's divinity in which the faithful see him as one with the Father, there is a concomitant tendency in the Middle Ages to view the Church chiefly as a sovereign. While the early Christians viewed the Church primarily as the Mother of her children, the faithful to whom she gives life in grace, the Christians of the Middle Ages interpret "Church" not so much as mother and nourisher but increasingly as leader and commander. With the maternal conceptualization receding into the background, the temporal and organizational aspect of the Church advances to the foreground.[21]

One of the most important consequences of this tendency to view the Church as a temporal power with its juridical-hierarchial apparatus was to emphasize the separation between clergy and laity. This development was further abetted by such circumstances as the clergy being the only ones capable of understanding Latin, the liturgical language of the Church. This language barrier proved to be an extremely difficult obstacle for the people to overcome and was certainly one of the principal reasons for the alienation of the people from the liturgy.

> Since the clergy (including the monks) were for the most part the only literate people and since it never occurred to them to translate the Bible into the language of the people, the liturgy in the West remained in the learned language of the clergy.[22]

Accustomed as they were to seeing absolute authority held in the hands of a small minority, the upper stratum of society, the Teutonic peoples had no trouble seeing the higher clergy as part of this group. New theological concepts were also responsible for exerting their influence on these movements. For instance, originally the faithful were seen as offering the sacrifice with the priest: "*qui tibi offerunt hoc sacrificium laudis*"; now, however, the priest at the altar is seen primarily as the one who offers the sacrifice for the people: "*pro quibus tibi offerimus.*"[23] The priest, surrounded by his assistants, is the only one allowed to enter the sanctuary in order to offer the sacrifice. The altar begins to move farther and farther away from the people into the rear of the apse and the priest now begins to say the prayers of the Canon in a low voice.[24]

Due to a series of complex factors, some of which have already been discussed, the altar assumed a new position which in turn affected the rearrangement of the sanctuary area of the church. The celebrant and the liturgical choir now were situated at the front of the altar interposed between the people and the altar. The faithful now found themselves that much farther removed from the altar. Soon great screens were erected at the entrance to the chancel which often prevented them from seeing the rite. Unable to see the rite and no longer able to understand its language, the people were forced to resort to private devotions in order to involve themselves to the best of their ability. While this rearrangement of the altar began in monastic churches, it soon was copied in parish churches all over northern Europe and remained in vogue until after the Reformation with the advent of the Baroque period.[25]

To a great extent, the concept of the clergy and the faithful as a holy people equally loved by God is no longer maintained. The clergy now becomes the chief and privileged representative of the Church while the corporate and public character of worship which was such an integral part of the life of early Christianity, now begins to disappear.

> It may indeed be wondered whether one of the first factors which led to the quiet medieval idea that the clergy celebrated the liturgy for the faithful, and even instead of them, but not with them, was not the removal of the clergy to an apse outside the community. This idea must have become irresistible when the altar itself was brought to this new and purely clerical sanctuary, so that the whole liturgy now took place, from the point of view of the faithful, behind the altar. To look at it from afar was now all they could do. The celebration had now ceased altogether to be theirs.[26]

As a logical consequence of these developments, the spiritual nature of the Church becomes somewhat obscured and a proper understanding of the life of grace for the individual Christian suffers accordingly. Despite the fact that people continued to feel obliged to receive the sacraments, that children continued to be baptized, that people continued to be blessed, and that the number of Christians living at that time in God's grace was presumably no less than in former times, the loss of the Christian's sense of sanctity was significant. From the ninth to the eleventh century the prayer literature reflects a negative attitude which seems prevalent at the time. Such negative themes as self-accusation, confession of personal unworthiness and sin dominated the prayer texts of the period.

Appreciation of Baptism, a sense of the objective sanctity which re-makes the being of a Christian, which we receive as a share of God's holiness through Baptism and the other sacraments, which remains with us despite all the wretchedness of frail human nature so long as we avoid mortal sin, all this seems to have vanished. Men seem to be preoccupied with clinging to moral goodness, with attaining a moral heroism raising them well above the average. The supernatural world has receded: this world is to the fore.[27]

With this point of view, people become less and less inclined to go to communion and must be urged to receive at least annually. This attitude cannot be attributed solely to the neglect of the faithful but principally to the tension that had been permitted to grow between the awesomeness, holiness and sublimity of the Blessed Sacrament and the sinfulness and unworthiness of the recipient. The early Christian concept of the Eucharist as the Christian's daily bread, which he approached with joy, confidence and frequency as the obvious consummation of the Holy Sacrifice has now radically changed. Thus, by the turn of the twelfth century, a new relationship to the Eucharist surfaces, one in which the Christian who formerly approached the Eucharist now withdraws from it. Because of this feeling of unapproachableness, the faithful now view the Sacrament from a distance and in this manner adore It devoutly.

From this development derive various practices: the elevation of the Species at the Consecration; exposition of the Sacrament upon the altar; carrying the Sacrament in solemn procession; and other forms of devotion. The object is not the use of the Sacrament but its cult; for, as popular meditation loves to think, it is God whom man confronts in prayer. The resulting forms may, indeed, be on the whole quite legitimate, an enrichment of a Eucharistic piety derived from another source, and ultimately capable of integration with it; but it still remains true, that until that integration was accomplished these forms represented a deviation from the original meaning of the Sacrament: and a major factor which set off this deviation was the state of Christological thought, still affected by defensive polemic and not yet having attained balanced expression.[28]

On the eve of the Reformation the Middle Ages were admittedly no longer a time of blossoming in the life of the Church. Quite the contrary, it was a time of notable decline and decay, a prelude to an extensive collapse. Nonetheless, judging from the general state of the Church at that time, things were not as bad as one might think.

Despite these developments, we find that the worship of God was carried out everywhere with great splendor on Sundays and feast days. All work ceased and civil sanctions ensured that the Sabbath rest was maintained. The Cathedral Church with its canons and clergy continued to be the center of the liturgical life of the Church.[29]

Magnificent church buildings were a reflection of the faithful's zeal for the worship of God. The end of the Middle Ages witnessed the building of most of the churches in South Germany and Austria. These churches betray specific architectural characteristics which despite renovation during the Baroque period continue to proclaim their earlier derivation. Though the towns and cities of the Middle Ages were relatively small, magnificent Gothic cathedrals and ministers arose everywhere thanks to the zeal of the faithful and the joyous alacrity with which the burghers gratuitously contributed to their construction. These magnificent structures were not only considered houses of God; they also added to the prestige of the town or city of which they were the greatest ornament and which their arched structures and majestic, pointed towers advertised from afar. "They were for the cities of the Middle Ages what temples were for those of antiquity."[30]

Speaking quantitatively, we can say that at the end of the Middle Ages there existed a high level of liturgical life. It was, however, a period of excessive development which led to very unhealthy conditions for liturgical worship. In some towns, not taking into consideration religious houses or monasteries, the clergy represented a high percentage of the population, as high as one in twenty of the population. To cathedrals and collegiate churches of the period, there were present not only the clergy necessary to maintain the solemn liturgy but also a large number of altar-priests, "whose only obligation was to offer a low Mass daily and to recite the Divine Office."[31]

The average person shared in the wealth of liturgical life by whatever endowment he could give toward the support of the clergy and the building and furnishing of the great churches. Despite this sharing, however, the liturgy itself continued to remain primarily a clerical function. Toward the end of the Middle Ages a tension developed between the laity and the clergy, especially the higher clergy, which became generally characteristic of church life. This strain was greatly augmented by the immense wealth of the clergy accrued through the ages from the many legacies and offerings of the rich.[32] All of this wealth had transformed the Church into the greatest landed proprietor in the world, and in Germany alone it owned over one-third of the land. Aside from its great wealth, the clergy also jealously guarded its prestigious position and the many privileges which went with it, an attitude which certainly worsened the situation and which most likely helped to foster that socialistic feeling which eventually expressed itself violently in the Peasant's War.[33]

Toward the end of the Middle Ages, despite the devotion of the people and their presence at worship, liturgy remained primarily a function of the clergy. This state of affairs received very clear expression in the collegiate churches and parishes as well with the erection of rood-screens. These screens were built to set off the area where the clergy carried out the sung office and the solemn liturgy from the main body of the church where the people were assembled. The choir stalls which had separated the choir from the nave, were originally transformed into a low barrier which gradually grew into a galleried structure dividing the monastic part of the church, the choir, from that of the laity, the nave.[34] Eventually, after further development, this screen was elaborated into a type of stage and called a *lectionarium* or lectern, upon which the choir could assemble. In the final analysis, the people were now further separated from the main altar by a wall. "The screen itself, at least in collegiate churches, came to be a wall, with only a central door leaving a scanty vision of what was happening inside but barring almost completely the people in the nave from any possibility of participation."[35]

Having been effectively cut off from the high altar of the church and the chief service which took place there, a second, and more generally, a third altar was set up in front of the screen in the nave. This altar was called the "people's altar" or "Crucifix altar" because of the crucifix mounted above it; and although these altars were not generally used for the public celebration of the liturgy but for private Masses, they nevertheless did offer the people the possibility of a more proximate approach to the Eucharistic Mysteries.[36]

Whatever Mass they attended, however, the people remained as nothing more than spectators inasmuch as the liturgical language remained Latin and consequently unintelligible to them. As for the readings, which for the most part were proclaimed facing away from the people, since the faithful could not readily understand them, they regarded them as symbolic representations of God's Word being preached to them. Slowly but surely, the clerical choir also assumed more and more unto itself so that soon even the simple chants of the Ordinary, which at one time were sung by the laity, were now sung by the choir. Eventually the choir is bolstered by musically trained laity and the church choir is born. These choirs, assembled upon the lectern, soon become very accomplished and increasingly adopt polyphonic music which the average person could not participate in if he wanted to. All of this was certainly an enrichment of the liturgy from one point of view, but from another it added to the growing estrangement of the liturgy from the people. In effect, there was nothing in which the people could have meaningfully participated in any longer—they had become dumb.[37]

The architecture of the Church continued to reflect in its own way the conditions that prevailed in the worship of the Church. When in early Christian times, the liturgy was more of a communal event, the principal altar stood on a raised platform located between the sanctuary and the nave, easily accessible to all. Now as conditions changed and the laity became less and less involved in the liturgy, the principal altar became drawn farther and farther away from the people into the rear of the apse. It is true, that in spite of the objections of the Synod of Mainz in 1351, its place was eventually usurped by a multitude of side altars required for the growing number of priests in the monasteries, who for many reasons desired to celebrate Mass frequently.[38] At first, small chapels built within the church itself accommodated these side-altars and their private Masses. "But in the later Middle Ages there was such a disproportionate growth in the number of clergy that altars began to be dotted around almost anywhere in the church without any regard for the spatial conditions."[39]

Even though this proliferation of side-altars represented a new obstacle in the way of a truly corporate, divine worship, the liturgy was always performed most solemnly. Because there was no lack of clergy, divine worship was always performed with great ceremony; and since Carolingian times it always contained dramatic elements which appealed to the senses of the people, making the understanding of words for the most part unnecessary. This only served to make the liturgy more of an external action, strictly adhering to a prescribed ritual and making the people more and more passive bystanders.[40]

Several ways in which the people maintained some vestige of participation included the sermon and the offertory procession. Through the sermon they received instructions on the Word of God, a direct communication. By means of the offertory procession people went up to the altar and paid their subscription even though the appreciation of the real liturgical significance of these processions was being gradually lost. Ultimately people lost the concept that by making their offering they were thus sharing in a very tangible way in the sacrifice of Christ and were expressing a total surrender of their own hearts and wills to the will of the Father in, with, and through the Spirit of Christ. On the contrary, they seemed more preoccupied with obtaining a share in the fruits of the Mass for the repose of the soul of a loved one or for some other special intention. Again, it is very significant that at this time people only rarely approached the table of the Lord to receive communion. Therefore, it was not through the reception of communion but through the giving of material gift that people sought to earn a share in the fruits of the Mass, almost in an *ex opere operato* fashion.[41]

The thirteenth century witnessed a new development which greatly affected the evolution of the Eucharist and its relationship to the people. Immediately after the reading of the institution narrative at Mass, a new elevation of the Sacred Species was introduced in order that all the faithful might view the Sacred Host and adore it from afar. Through contemplation the faithful saw the raised Host as the source of temporal blessings and eternal rewards. This action soon became the center of the whole popular devotion of the Mass. Because of this development and the people's longing to adore the presence of the Savior in the raised Host, the faithful no longer wanted or did not dare to go to communion at Mass. The pastoral attitude of the clergy, which encouraged these developments, was certainly most responsible for the growth of this tendency and attitude on the part of the people.[42]

Since this elevation now seemed to be the focal point of the entire Mass, many people would simply leave the church after they had viewed the raised Host which in some contrived manner was able to be made visible despite the obstruction of the rood-screen. This was an abuse which the Church strongly condemned.

Yet it is to some extent understandable when one recalls that in many churches, apart from the entrance and exit procession of the clergy, the

Elevation was the only thing in the Mass visible to the people; and when one recalls further that usually the celebrating priest alone received Holy Communion.[43]

This new practice of elevating the Host spread rapidly, and by the end of the thirteenth century it was just about a universal practice in the West. Soon after, the elevation of the chalice was introduced but was not as universally practiced, apparently because one was able to see the Host at the first elevation but was not able to see the consecrated wine at the second.[44]

While we can certainly determine a formal Eucharistic movement in the Middle Ages, nevertheless, we can see that its ultimate purpose was not to foster participation in the Eucharist or to encourage more frequent reception of communion but only to advance the practice of the contemplation and veneration of the Blessed Sacrament from afar. "This may be considered as the beginning of the modern tendency to substitute a mere visualization for actual participation."[45]

Eventually, from this type of Eucharistic devotion sprang such practices as the exposition of the Blessed Sacrament during the entire Mass and the initiation of the Holy Hour. Groups of Christians form Confraternities whose specific purpose is to venerate the Blessed Sacrament, and this same Blessed Sacrament is now all too frequently carried about in processions on any and every pretext. As pious as these practices may have been, they also gave rise to several dangerous and superstitious ideas. The danger was that in venerating the Sacrament men would see it primarily as a means of obtaining earthly blessings. For instance, it was believed that a mere glimpse of the Sacred Host, especially at the moment of Consecration, would produce temporal benefits for the beholder. Some of the popular beliefs maintained that if the Sacred Host was viewed in the morning by one of the faithful, he would be protected throughout the day from such dire events as blindness, a sudden death, hunger and other such calamities. It was also maintained that while a man was attending Mass he did not age; and if the Mass was being said for the holy souls in purgatory, they did not suffer for the duration of the Mass. Another belief was that each time the Mass was offered a soul was freed from purgatory; and that food taken after Mass was especially more nourishing than food taken at other times. Many other similar beliefs were prevalent at the time.[46]

This type of thinking slowly but surely gained acceptance among the simple people. Soon it was held that as long as you were devoutly present at Mass, the effects would automatically accrue to you. The concept of sacrifice has now switched from the former idea of a gift offered to God by which the faithful Christian renders him honor and praise to one in which the Christian now receives gifts and benefits from God; the greatest gift of all offered by God to man in the Holy Sacrifice, the gift of his own Body and Blood in Communion is overlooked. The Mass now becomes more the mystery of God's descent to man, the mystery which man must merely look at and adore from a distance. Even on feast days participation in the Lord's table became an exception for the majority of the people; "already the Eucharist had not been our daily bread for a long time."[47]

The late Middle Ages also witnessed the introduction of symbolism as yet another way of viewing the Mass and the liturgy. Unfortunately, this development did not lead to a deeper, sacramental Christianity but to an allegorical interpretation of the Mass to provide meditation on the Passion of the Lord. This movement was exemplified by the medieval *Expositiones Missae* of which Amalarius (780–850) was the chief proponent. It displayed an overemphasis on the Divine Presence in the Holy Eucharist as well as an overly sentimental view of that same Presence.

> Both can be viewed as expressions of the tendency to be found in those sentimentally realistic explanations of the Mass in which it was taken for granted that the Mass was meant to reproduce the Passion of a kind of mimetic reproduction, each action of the Mass representing some action of the Passion itself: for example, the priest's moving from the Epistle side of the altar to the Gospel side being a representation of Jesus' journey from Pilate to Herod; or the Lavabo representing Pilate washing his hands. Aside from their intrinsic absurdity, such explanations served to dissolve the traditional conception of a sacramental presence into actions. As if the liturgy were aiming at reproducing materially and theatrically the acts by which we were saved, as if it intended to suggest not only the physical, but also a carnal presence of Our Lord to be grasped more by imagination than by faith.[48]

This misrepresentation of the liturgical mystery as just an allegorical reenactment of the Passion represents one of the last stages in the medieval tendency of placing excessive emphasis on the suffering humanity of Christ as well as the slow but certain disappearance of the concept of a truly sacramental liturgy, "this idea having already been buried under a merely sentimental and allegorical remembrance of the past, in the *Expositiones Missae*."[49]

The principal characteristics of this entire movement are found in the following description:

> ... A spiritual climate of very low intellectual caliber, a symbolism which is well-intentioned but mostly divorced from the actual rite of the Eucharist, a concentration of the physical and human details of Christ's life, and, if we include the many abuses as also characteristics of the period, a swaying of "attitude" toward the Eucharist as an object rather than an action, as a thing to be studied in what one might call philosophically "physical categories," and an attitude in which the consciousness of belonging to a community has more or less evaporated.[50]

Consequently, in relation to the degree of worship and awe rendered to the Eucharist in this exaggerated manner there is a proportionate lack of attention and reverence rendered to the Eucharist in its more meaningful aspect as a sacrificial meal.[51]

The dual factors of a faulty Eucharistic theology shallowly grounded in a bed of arbitrary but well-intentioned symbolism and a popular piety involved with superstitious practices made it only a matter of time before some extremists would go beyond the symbolism and superstition and transform the Eucharist itself into a mere symbol. These excesses fostered Eucharistic controversies, and these controversies in turn effected many changes. In the early Church the practice of venerating the Eucharist outside of Mass was unknown.[52] However, because of the human need for symbols and the concentration on the suffering humanity of Christ, this practice was gradually changed. Already in the eleventh century, in reacting against the heresy of Berengar of Tours (c. 999–1088), Cluny, Canterbury and the Cistercians were promoting the practice of devotion to the Blessed Sacrament.[53] In time, this helped to promote new research on the theology of the Real Presence and fostered a renewed interest in attempting to establish the exact moment of Consecration—that is, at what moment during Mass was the bread and wine actually transformed into the Body and Blood of Christ.

> The cultus of the Blessed Sacrament, which followed as a reaction from the heretical teaching of Berengar, became increasingly accentuated in the succeeding centuries of the Middle Ages. Respect to the reserved Sacrament was inculcated, and instructions were issued by synods and bishops regarding the safe custody of the Eucharist.[54]

The usual place set aside for the safe custody of the Eucharist was some recess, cupboard or aumbry, sometimes set fairly high up in the wall of the church, most usually on the Gospel side, and secured by iron bars or grill. These practices were by no means universal for there certainly was no one set rule, followed everywhere, for the reservation of the Eucharist. That "suspension" of the Blessed Sacrament was universally practiced is an erroneous assumption. This method of using a recess, cupboard or aumbry set into the wall left much to be desired; one of the most common objections to this practice was that these locations were most usually damp, a condition that was certainly not conducive to the preservation of the reserved Species. One of the solutions to this problem, as practiced in the Low Countries, Germany and the Slavic lands in communion with Rome, was the building of "Sacrament Houses" which, due to their costliness, were only available to wealthy churches and not to country parishes who had to solve the problem in another, less expensive way.[55] These richly ornamented towers, which originally stood apart from the altar, continued to be used until the Renaissance when they were greatly reduced in size and for the most part relocated to a central position on the main altar.[56] The presence of a fixed tabernacle upon the altar, as we understand it today, first made its appearance during the Italian Renaissance and began to spread elsewhere only after the Council of Trent.[57] "It remained for the Goths to erect their towering reredoses on top of the altar and for the pseudo-Goths of the nineteenth century to embed the tabernacle in them, for the altar to lose almost all semblance of what it once had been and was intended to be."[58]

As the Middle Ages declined, that part of Church life which maintained its vitality and meaning for the people was the celebration of the Christian festivals. The Christian accepted with open heart the meaning of each and every festival, and he celebrated them with great enthusiasm and zeal. The pictorial art of the age clearly demonstrates this attitude as the artists' principal subjects, aside from the paintings of certain saints, patrons and benefactors, were the Christmas and Easter themes. Late Gothic art produced countless variations of the Nativity scene as well as all the events surrounding it. However, the most richly portrayed topic is that of the Paschal Mystery beginning with the Passion of Christ and ending with his Resurrection and Ascension.[59]

In fact it can be said that the entire social order was seen as contained within a supernatural order, an order made highly accessible to man through the wonder and pageantry of the liturgy. Therefore, despite the many corruptions, there was a kind of flowering of liturgical life on the eve of the Reformation which even included the participation of the faithful. However, it was not an authentic flowering but a forced one. "It was the flowering of Autumn . . . the last branching out, the late consequences of ancient tradition . . . often mere empty play. There was a mighty facade, and behind it, a great emptiness."[60]

In summary, therefore, in spite of the people's great love for the liturgy and the frequency with which it was celebrated, and despite the many developments in the area of Eucharistic theology, the liturgy was not what it should have been. Its great deficiency was that it was no longer understood by the people in its sacramental depth, an area which was essentially forgotten. The Christian mystery had lost its relevancy for the here and now and was almost always viewed as a mere memorial of past events to be meditated on through some form of popular devotion.[61]

Unfortunate too is the fact that the Church of the late Middle Ages was often represented by many ambitious men who through their lust for power, their avarice and the bad example of their lives contributed a great deal toward transforming the Church into a predominantly earthly, sociological entity. As a result, the Church began to abdicate her rightful position in religious and liturgical life and continued to lose her identity as the community of the faithful.[62]

This condition was graphically revealed in late Gothic Church architecture. "It is in this period that we have an instance of a fitting adaptation of means to ends. It combined the taste of the time for big altar-pieces with the uncompromising, overruling assertion of the Sacrament as the very principle of life of the church building itself."[63] With the demand of the guilds and of prominent families for their own altar and private worship, churches now begin to establish a multitude of private chapels. The Sunday and feast day liturgies, at one time such great community services, now begin to lose their attraction for the people. These developments could have been the result of the attempts of the new pastoral orders to have their own liturgical services accepted as fully as the regular parish liturgies. These practices further obscure the idea of community and eventually result in the prevailing notion that the Sunday obligation need not be fulfilled in one's own parish church but anywhere and at any time. From the fourteenth to the sixteenth century, synod after synod firmly opposed this practice and continued to maintain that the faithful were obliged to fulfill their Sunday obligations in their own parish church. In the end, however, Rome decided in favor of the people's freedom of choice. This right was affirmed by a decree of Pope Leo X in 1517 and once again the idea of community was dealt a severe blow.[64]

During this period there was another particular point of dissolution which was affecting the very heart of ecclesiastical and liturgical life. Public worship as the norm and food of the spiritual life of the faithful has the principal function of helping man to grasp as effectively as possible the mystery of Christ. This is achieved through the wise use of signs and symbols whose outward forms help man to participate more fully and meaningfully in worship. But these outward forms have their limitations and in their function they can only help man to understand more fully and to assimilate more deeply the liturgical mysteries.

> But as we advance into the medieval centuries these outward forms take on the character of an end in themselves, and hence the knowledge of the liturgy becomes more superficial. A great appreciation of its outward manifestations is felt; but its content, the reality of the mystery of Christ in the liturgy and in the Christian life, is already far from the minds of the faithful. Little by little, the theological basis is being forgotten, while the love of everything that arouses the feelings is increasing. What is sought is not so much the participation in the sacramental life and the understanding of the mysteries, but the material apparatus of worship and the kind of devotion that affects the senses.[65]

Consequently, while the basic faith of the people is not destroyed, it is a faith no less rooted in peripheral things.

> Veneration of the saints and their relics, genuine or fake, is often quite unrestrained. Protections and blessings are sought in ever-new ways: the rituals become full of new benedictions. Confraternities are founded and new devotions spring up all around. Religious life becomes more and more complicated. A growing insecurity and many-sided discontent is apparent everywhere. There is no longer any close connection between altar and people. It was very easy for Luther to strike a staggering blow at this system.[66]

Thus, at the end of the Middle Ages this type of extreme liturgical decadence helped very much to foster the birth of Protestantism.

The liturgy had ceased to be what it was meant to be in the lives of the people, for the altar and the worshipping community were no longer one.

Notes

[1] Jean-Remy Palanque, *The Dawn of the Middle Ages*, trans. Dom Finbarr Murphy (New York: Hawthorne Books, 1960), p. 110.

[2] Josef Jungmann, *Pastoral Liturgy* (New York: Herder and Herder, 1962), p. 9.

[3] *Ibid.* pp. 15–16.

[4] *Ibid.*

[5] Johannes Quasten, *Patrology* (Utrecht: Spectrum Publishers, 1966), III, pp. 1–13.

[6] *Ibid.*

[7] R. Kevin Seasoltz, *The House of God*, (New York: Herder and Herder, 1963), p. 104.

[8] Josef Jungmann, *The Mass of the Roman Rite*, trans. Francis A. Brunner (New York: Benziger Brothers. Inc., 1955), I, pp. 38–39, 328.

[9] Friedrich Heer, *The Medieval World*, trans. Janet Sondheimer, (New York: The New American Library, 1962), p. 199.

[10] *The Oxford Dictionary of the Christian Church*, ed. F. L. Cross (London: Oxford University Press, 1958), p. 358.

[11] L. Eisenhofer, J. Lechner, *The Liturgy of the Roman Rite*, trans. A.J. and E.F. Peeler, ed. H.E. Winstone (New York: Herder and Herder, 1961), p. 123.

[12] Jungmann, *Pastoral Liturgy*, pp. 44–45.

[13] *Ibid.*, pp. 45–47.

[14] Heer, *op. cit.*, pp. 389–390.

[15] Jungmann, *Pastoral Liturgy*, p. 48.

[16] *Ibid.*, pp. 48–49.

[17] Josef Jungmann, *The Good News Yesterday and Today*, trans. and ed. William A. Huesman (New York: W. H. Sadlier, Inc., 1962), pp. 60–61.

[18] A. Verheul, *Introduction to the Liturgy*, (Collegeville: The Liturgical Press, 1968), p. 143.

[19] Louis Bouyer, *Liturgical Piety*, (Notre Dame: University of Notre Dame Press, 1954), p. 42.

[20] Jungmann, *Pastoral Liturgy*, pp. 57–58

[21] *Ibid.*, pp. 58–59.

[22] J.D. Crichton, "A Historical Sketch of the Roman Liturgy," *True Worship*, ed. Lancelot Sheppard (Baltimore: The Helicon Press, 1963), p. 63.

[23] Jungmann, *The Mass of the Roman Rite*, II, pp. 166–169.

[24] Louis Bouyer, *Eucharist*, (Notre Dame: University of Notre Dame Press, 1968), pp. 366–379.

[25] Crichton, *op. cit.*

[26] Louis Bouyer, *Liturgy and Architecture*, (Notre Dame: University of Notre Dame Press, 1967), pp. 59–60.

[27] Jungmann, *Pastoral Liturgy*, p. 62.

[28] *Ibid.*, p. 63.

[29] *Ibid.*, p. 64.

[30] Henri Pirenne, *Medieval Cities*, trans. Frank D. Halsey (New York: Doubleday and Company, Inc., 1956), pp. 149–150.

[31] Jungmann, *op. cit.*, p. 66.

[32] John P. Dolan, *History of the Reformation*, (New York: Desclée Company, 1965), pp. 77–78.

[33] Jungmann, *op. cit.*, p. 67.

[34] Eisenhofer and Lechner, *op. cit.*, p. 125.

[35] Bouyer, *Liturgy and Architecture*, pp. 70–71.

[36] *Ibid.*, p. 80.

[37] Jungmann, *Pastoral Liturgy*, p. 68.

[38] Eisenhofer and Lechner, *op. cit.*, p. 122; B. J. Kidd, *The Later Medieval Doctrine of the Eucharistic Sacrifice*, (London: S.P.C.K., 1958), pp. 40–41.

[39] Josef A. Jungmann, *Public Worship*, (Collegeville: The Liturgical Press, 1957), p. 61.

40 Jungmann, *Pastoral Liturgy,* pp. 68–69.

41 *Ibid.,* p. 70.

42 Bouyer, *Eucharist,* p. 381.

43 Johannes Wagner, "Liturgical Art and the Care of Souls," *The Assisi Papers,* (Collegeville: The Liturgical Press, 1957), p. 64.

44 Adrian Fortescue, *The Mass—A Study of the Roman Liturgy,* (New York: Longmans, Green and Company, 1937), pp. 340–341.

45 Bouyer, *Liturgy and Architecture,* p. 72.

46 Adolf Franz, *Die Messe in Deutschen Mittelalter,* (Freiburg-im-Breisgau, 1902), pp. 46 ff.

47 Jungmann, *The Mass of the Roman Rite,* I, p. 84.

48 Bouyer, *Liturgical Piety,* p. 16.

49 Bouyer, *Liturgical Piety,* p. 42.

50 Theodore Westow, *The Variety of Catholic Attitudes,* (New York: Herder and Herder, 1963), pp. 40–41.

51 Josef A. Jungmann, *The Place of Christ in Liturgical Prayer,* trans. A. Peeler (New York: Alba House, 1965), pp. 262–263.

52 J. Braun, *Der christliche Altar in seiner geistlichen Entwicklung,* (Munich: Koch and Company, 1924), II, p. 574.

53 B. Neunheuser, *L'Eucharistie—Au Moyen Age et A L'Epoque Moderne,* trans. A Liefooghe (Paris: Les Editions du Cerf, 1966), pp. 46–51.

54 Archdale A. King, *Eucharistic Reservation in the Western Church,* (New York: Sheed and Ward, 1965), p. 55.

55 Bishop, *op. cit.,* p. 36.

56 Bouyer, *Liturgy and Architecture,* p. 85.

57 E. Maffei, *La Reservation Eucharistique jusqu' à la Renaissance,* (Bruxelles: Eds Vromant S.A., 1942), pp. 123–128.

58 Crichton, *True Worship,* p. 70.

59 Jungmann, *Pastoral Liturgy,* p. 73.

60 *Ibid.,* pp. 77-78.

61 Kidd, *op. cit.,* pp. 34–39.

[62] Jungmann, *Pastoral Liturgy*, pp. 78–79.

[63] Edmund Bishop, "On the History of the Christian Altar," *Downside Review*, (July 1905), pp. 154–182.

[64] Jungmann, *The Mass of the Roman Rite*, I, pp.249–250.

[65] Gabriel M. Braso, *Liturgy and Spirituality,* trans. Leonard J. Doyle (Collegeville: The Liturgical Press, 1960), p. 38.

[66] Jungmann, *Pastoral Liturgy*, pp. 79–80.

Chapter III

The Influence of Medieval Eucharistic Theology and Piety Upon the Altar

Up until now we have seen a brief history of the Christian altar in the Western Church through the Middle Ages into the beginning of the Baroque period. Subsequently, we examined some of the major trends of Eucharistic theology in the popular vein during the Middle Ages and have attempted to show briefly how these factors have had their own effect upon the altar: its significance, its location and its decoration in the Christian Church during the Medieval era. We realize that we cannot draw any universal, simplistic transference between Eucharistic theology, popular devotion and the Christian altar precisely because of the great divergences between various cultures and nationalities and many other inconsistencies due to a multiplicity of complex reasons. For example, "the disposition of the chancel barring the people from any access to the altar, however prevalent, was never universal in the Middle Ages."[1] Nevertheless, we do feel that, generally speaking, this connection can be illustrated in many instances. For this reason, the present research in this chapter proposes to examine several Gothic cathedrals of the Middle Ages (the Gothic cathedral being the fullest embodiment of the Christian civilization of the Middle Ages),[2] and will further attempt to demonstrate concretely in these edifices a verification of the effects of Eucharistic theology and popular piety upon the altar and its relationship to the people. There will be of necessity a repetition of many of the things already stated in Chapters I and II in order to better organize and summarize the entire issue involved in this final chapter.

With the victory of Constantine over Maxentius in the year 312 at the Milvian Bridge, the Christians hailed the cessation of their sufferings and the success of Constantine as a victory for God and a clear demonstration of his over-ruling providence. By reason of the continuing triumph of the Church over paganism and the rapidly increasing number of Christians, there arose the necessity of larger buildings for worship.

Prior to this, the Eucharistic liturgy of the early Church was celebrated in the ordinary home. Although at first these were private homes, they later more frequently became community property altered to serve the liturgical needs of the community. So at Dura Europos (c. 232), a partition was removed in order to establish a special room for the Eucharistic celebration, while as late as the year 303 a house was established in Cirta where the Christians ordinarily met for worship. However, as we have previously stated, with the Edict of Milan in the year 313 and the subsequent growth of congregations, the buildings soon proved inadequate and special buildings became necessary.[3] For the early Romans the architectual style of these new, more spacious churches is usually called the Latin Basilica. While this term ordinarily designated for them a large hall or a grand public or private edifice, by the fourth or fifth centuries the term was usually applied to churches.[4]

> The basilica introduced no new architectual elements, since its form was determined by the functional synthesis of the five basic requirements of Christian worship: (1) a large assembly room destined to house the entire community, hierarchically arranged about an axis; (2) the cathedra of the presiding bishop; (3) the ambo for the reading of the Holy Scriptures, from here also the singing of the psalms was conducted; (4) the baptismal font which, in view of the baptismal ritual, stood outside the assembly room; and (5) the table for the Eucharist.[5]

Many features characterizing the early Christian basilica were adopted from the synagogue and its worship. But the feature which ultimately distinguished the Christian church from the synagogue and differentiated it from the pagan temples was the table of the Lord upon which the Eucharistic banquet was celebrated.[6]

In the West, the basilica church-type was to prevail as the principal church building for some seven hundred years.[7] As a result of the complications introduced by the increasing intricacy of the liturgy, the original, simple arrangement of the basilica was later modified. The dispositions were modified first of all in those basilicas which contained a *memoria*. In the beginning, the *memoria* stood apart from the basilica itself; but, by the time the Basilica of Saint

Peter was erected, the *memoria* was incorporated into the church edifice itself. For hundreds of years the side walls of the basilica or the side of the apse were the normal erection sites for *memoriae* and *martyria* which in turn were surrounded by the ordinary mausolea of rich and pious citizens. This custom prevailed in the West up to the Carolingian period. Further complications arose when the martyr's tomb and the altar were combined. In the cemetery *memoria* located outside the city walls, this became an obvious development. However, this became a general practice when the relics of the martyrs began to be transferred from the cemeteries to the churches themselves. A third complication developed from the formation of the clerical choir and the consequent need of permanent seats for the increasing number of *continentes* or monks who sang the psalms daily in the basilica.[8]

Upon examination of the early basilicas, we find that they were generally composed of three principal elements: the atrium, the nave, and the chancel. The atrium was a forecourt attached to the basilica. Open to the exterior through a single door, it consisted of a colonnaded quadrangle with a fountain in the center used for ritual ablutions. It was connected with the interior of the basilica by what was called the narthex or portico which later evolved into the vestibule of the modern church.

The nave was that part of the basilica which stretched from the main front up to the chancel and choir and which was assigned to the laity. This normally vast rectangular space, about twice as long as it was wide, was usually divided from the side aisles by two rows of parallel columns or pillars and from the sanctuary by a screen. Normally higher than the other two sections, the middle section had windows which opened to the outside. A fenced-off area for the *schola cantorum* was located before the chancel in the middle of the nave. The Sacred Scriptures were read and the psalms were sung at an ambo which was located outside the balustrade surrounding the choir.[9]

The chancel was that area of the church which was located at the opposite end of the nave from the atrium. Raised slightly above the floor of the basilica, it terminated in a semi-circular section called the apse. The bishop's throne, flanked on either side by simple stone benches for the clergy, was located at the very rear of the apse. The altar, which was usually a simple stone table resting under a *ciborium* supported by four columns, was situated between the bishop's throne and the people in the nave. It is most likely that the altar was similarly located in the house-churches. The faithful usually assembled on either side of the choir with the men on the right and the women on the left. Being so proximate to the altar, they were thus able to share intimately in the liturgical action which the bishop celebrated facing his people. The hierarchical arrangement of the church was the most likely reason why the altar faced the people in the Latin basilica. Since the bishop's throne stood facing all the people, it was natural for him whenever he approached the altar to stand at the side closest to the throne. The bishop, as the mediator between God and His people, always exercised his role as chief liturgist for the worshipping community.[10]

The origin of the Christian basilica has been an archeological problem that has been very much debated and yet never conclusively settled. It is, nonetheless certain that when the Christian basilicas did appear on the scene in the fourth century, they immediately appeared as well-planned, beautifully functional churches. Within these churches, under the direction of the bishop and his priests, the worshipping community was able to assemble in well ordered fashion to celebrate the divine liturgy as a true *plebs sancta*.[11]

> In the early church the deliberate effort was made to divide up the functions of worship among as many people as possible. The bishop was when possible the celebrant, and was surrounded by his priests who (at least at Rome) concelebrated with him; the deacons, headed by the archdeacon, and the subdeacons had their share in the reading of the lessons and the ceremonial of the altar: chanters and choir, acolytes and doorkeepers all had their place; the people too had their share in the action, in the offering of the gifts and the kiss of peace and the communion.[12]

This type of communal liturgy in which all the different orders of the Church had their own proper function to perform was accommodated in the design of these first church buildings. The twelfth century basilica of Saint Clement in Rome is an unusually good illustration of what was probably the typical layout of the fourteenth century basilica. The Eucharistic liturgy took place in a rectangular hall with an apse at the east end. In the very rear of the apse, flanked by seats for his presbyters, the bishop's throne was located. Further out from the east end of the church and the bishop's throne, the altar was situated under a suspended canopy or *ciborium*. For the liturgy of the Word, the ministers remained seated in the apse, and the bishop preached from his throne. At the offertory, the ministers approached the altar, and the gifts which the laity presented were placed on the altar by the deacons. During the service the bishop and his concelebrants faced the people across the altar. The choir or *schola cantorum* was stationed in the center of the church in an area adjoining the sanctuary and surrounded by low *cancelli* or balustrades. On either side of this enclosure, there was an ambo from which the lessons were read. This type of layout expressed in true biblical fashion that the Eucharist is not the act of one or of a few individuals but rather the action of the entire priestly community. The altar is very close to the people of God and as the table of the Lord remains central to the worship of the Church with the Church gathered around it for the celebration of the Eucharistic banquet.[13]

It should be quite obvious that this particular layout of the basilica served in an exemplary way the basic needs of the Roman liturgy. Dogmatic concerns about priesthood and about the material presence of Christ in the Eucharist—which would continue to preoccupy the Church from then on—were faithfully translated into this type of structure. This trend of thought slowly but surely developed and dominated Catholic thinking for centuries to come.

> The doctrine of transubstantiation is inconceivable apart from the belief in a holy place where the Divinity is present by means of the sacrament, and the idea of a priestly class privileged over against the lay members of the community. The material presence of the Divinity in sacred places and objects, which are thus accorded respect and veneration, means that they may be approached only by ecclesiastical officials who have been initiated into the sacred mystery.[14]

Toward the end of the Middle Ages a complete transformation had occurred, and the liturgy of the West had lost its essential character as a communal action. With the growth of the Church and its concomitant expansion from the cities into the country, the bishop could no longer officiate as the principal celebrant at the Sunday Eucharist for all his people. The bishop now had to delegate the presbyter, his former deputy, as his official representative so that the presbyter soon came to be regarded as the normal celebrant of the liturgy. The people took less and less of an active role in the liturgy and soon became mere spectators. Their former roles now usurped by the clergy, the laity communicated sacramentally only infrequently. The later Middle Ages witnessed the normal type of celebration to be one at which a priest, assisted by a server, celebrated Mass for the community. The practice of concelebration as well as the practice of diversity of functions had virtually disappeared, and the ordinary Christian now saw the Mass as a wonderful, awefilled, mysterious ceremony performed for him and no longer with him. Now pushed further and further away from the Eucharistic action, the people lost all sense of communal participation and must now occupy themselves with devotions generally unrelated to the liturgy taking place, gazing in awe and adoration upon the elevated Sacred Species. The people must now be content with seeing rather than doing, and the emphasis has switched from offering and the reception of communion to passivity and the elevation.[15]

The actual setting of the liturgy became a faithful reflection of the state of the liturgy. As the liturgy was transformed from the communal liturgy of the fourth century to the low Mass of the fourteenth century, we see these changes mirrored in the liturgical setting. The priest was transferred from behind the altar to a position in front of it, while the altar itself was relocated to a position against the east wall of the apse. With the altar now occupying the traditional site of the bishop's throne, the throne is moved out to a position between the altar and the people. From the sixth century on, the practice of placing the altar against the rear of the east wall in parish churches takes place with increasing frequency. "But we know also that it was from about the year 1000 onwards that outside Rome the practice of celebrating Mass with the priest's back to the congregation became the general rule."[16]

As the liturgical role of the faithful diminished in importance during the Middle Ages, the importance of the clergy was proportionately magnified. The Eucharist became the exclusive domain of the priest, who by virtue of his orders now celebrated in relative isolation from the offering of the whole Christian community. This development is ultimately responsible for effecting the sudden multiplication of side altars in the church building effectively deemphasizing the centrality of the main altar.[17]

As a result of this, in about the eighth century, the celebration of "private" Masses became the rule and not the exception. This led to the eventual exaggeration of the ninth century when many priests would offer Mass several times in the same day. Also, with the medieval cult of saints, these numerous altars more often than not served as the provision of a base for the many reliquaries housed in each cathedral church.[18]

It was the monastic church which had originally adopted a layout effectively separating the church into two sections: one section (the chancel) being reserved for the clergy and the other (the nave) being assigned to the laity. Both sections were separated from each other by a screen of sorts. This type of layout was soon also adopted by parish churches and down through the ages eventually came to be accepted not only by the architects of the Gothic revival but also by most people as the normal or traditional layout of a church. This plan was an extremely good one for the late Middle Ages, for it was functionally consonant with the clericalized society and liturgy of its day. But it was the product of a theological and liturgical revolution which reflected a far different understanding of the Church as attested to by the church buildings of an earlier age.[19]

Due to this significant shift in understanding, the gulf between the clergy and the laity widened. The fourth century bears witness to the Church's recognition of the theological distinction of functions within the Christian liturgy. Beginning with the bishop and all his ministers and concluding with the ordinary Christian, we find that all have their own proper liturgical functions to perform, both in the church and outside it. As a highly organic structure, the Church is hierarchical in its composition. The late Middle Ages, however, finds the Church very much identified with many aspects of society as a whole. The sociological categories of clerk and layman eventually replaced the traditional concept of the distinction of functions within the Church. People lost their self-concept as active participants in Christ's priestly and redemptive mission. Consequently, they no longer considered themselves as members of the priesthood of Christ. Rather, in the face of rising clericalism, members of the laity are reckoned as laymen in a purely negative sense, being evaluated as inferior to clerics, as outsiders, as non-experts. Effectively separated from the altar, the layman of the Middle Ages accepted his passive role and was thus excluded from any active role in the liturgy.[20]

These developments are clearly attested to in the overall structure of the cathedral of the Middle Ages which graphically portrays in solid and unambiguous terms the pre-eminence that priest and altar enjoyed in the Christian life. Thus these magnificent cathedrals, with their marvelously wrought sanctuaries, provide mankind with an extremely faithful record of all the currents of the religious activity of that period. As the faithful recorder of these trends, the cathedral can be seen as the apogee of man's expressive recounting in stone and mortar of the effects of these trends in his own life. The design of these structures is perfectly in tune with the penitential piety of the innumerable pilgrims forever coming and going and forever submissive to the liturgical directives of a multitude of clergy.

> The Gothic cathedral interior triumphs in the architecture of the choir, the supreme culmination of its structural and artistic possibilities, the architectual expression of a transcendent event and one which is constantly repeated, the celebration of the Mass at the High Altar in the sanctuary. If we seek the point of departure from which the substance of Gothic took shape, we must turn to the choir as the center of worship. There are Gothic cathedral interiors existing only as choirs, like those of Beauvais and Le Mans, which would be sufficient alone to explain the spirit and the power of the art of Gothic. In the classic cathedrals the walls of the nave direct the gaze to the choir, the exalted, unapproachable Holy of Holies, in which the meaning of the architecture is particularly concentrated. From the point of view of design, the architecture of the choir contained a host of special requirements, and the resource and skill with which these were fulfilled must arouse the highest admiration for the architects who worked on the cathedral sites. These special requirements are also a part of a French tradition in the form of the choir of large churches.[21]

The altar and its position and decoration in the cathedral is the product of this theological and liturgical revolution. It is generally located within the choir, which, like an island within the cathedral, "was raised a few steps from the nave and shut in on the other sides as well as toward the nave by huge stone screens, which were erected with great ornamentation and splendor."[22]

I shall now attempt to illustrate in several of the classic Gothic cathedrals of France how these forces had indeed affected the altar and its role as table of the Lord in the midst of his people. First of all, I would like to examine the Cathedral of Notre Dame of Paris.

Begun in 1163 by Maurice de Sully and completed in 1330, it is seen as the supreme jewel among those magnificent cathedrals with tribune galleries which date from the second half of the twelfth century. It was strongly influenced in design by Laon Cathedral but with the pattern somewhat simplified and enlarged. The most precious element of the new church was obviously the chancel, which was provided with as formidable an area as space would allow. Despite the spaciousness of the church, however, the centrally located chancel, flanked by a spacious double aisle, is a relatively narrow forty-three feet wide and one hundred and twenty-one feet long. In order to best accommodate the liturgy, this chancel was divided into two separate sections, much as it is today. The choir included the first four bays which housed the Chapter during the Mass. The far end of the chancel, which was separated from the choir proper (and the nave beyond the choir) by a flight of three steps, comprised the sanctuary itself, where the principal altar was located, and above which stretched a great semicircular vault of eight ogive ribs. The apse was composed of the double aisle that surrounded the sanctuary.[23]

When the building was completed early in the fourteenth century, the high altar, normally draped with precious fabrics on feast days, was then decorated with copper sheeting imbedded with polished uncut stones. A silver-gilt reredos showing the Annunciation and the Coronation of the Virgin, Saint Stephen and Saint Marcel, carved by Jean de Montpelier between 1320 and 1333 then replaced the golden frontal which had been a gift from Bishop Maurice de Sully. This same golden frontal was later sent to be melted down in order to raise money to help the king wage war against the Protestants. The shrine of Saint Marcel, made up of precious metals and surrounded by figurines, stood behind the main altar at the height of 16 feet 5 inches, housed by a sumptuous miniature temple guarded by angels. At the corners of the altar stood four copper pillars united by curtain-rods on which heavy tapestries were mounted. These same pillars were surmounted by enamelled and painted angels with their wings spread. The angels had been restored by Jean d'Orleans under the direction of Raymond du Temple in 1371. Directly behind the altar, there was a tall copper crozier bearing an angel carrying the *pyxidium* in which the Blessed Sacrament was placed. Below this a silver-gilt Virgin holds in her hands the reliquary containing the Virgin's girdle. Many shrines glittering with silver and gold and mounted on richly sculptured pedestals abounded in this area of the church.[24]

To the right of the altar are the seats of the celebrants and the deacons, completed in 1340 by a carpenter, Gautier Houel. The stone screen which separated the choir from the sanctuary was replaced by a copper screen, the work of the metal-founder Etienne Bavrillet, who completed it in 1595. On each side of the choir, carved wooden stalls were placed with their leather-decorated backs against the choir-screens. This was commenced on the north side by Pierre de Chelles from 1300 to 1318, who also erected the rood-screen, and continued on the south side by Jean Ravy from 1318 to 1344. The apsidal part was completed between 1344 and 1351 by Jean le Bouteiller. On the north and south walls, scenes from the childhood of Christ and the Appearances after the Resurrection are depicted. The rood-screen, showing scenes from the Passion and the Resurrection and remodelled and transformed several times, has disappeared. The story of the Patriarch Joseph, a forerunner of Christ, which was sculptured in high-relief in the apse at the expense of the Canon de Fayel, has likewise disappeared. The Canon, who died in 1344, also had the stained-glass windows of the chevet renewed. Once again, nothing remains of these.[25]

From this description we can readily see the ornateness of the main altar at the beginning of the fourteenth century. This ornateness included such things as a golden frontal, silver-gilt reredos, martyr shrine, a *ciborium* of four copper pillars at the corners of the altar, and many other precious decorations, and all was enclosed by an altar screen of rich, heavy tapestries. We also note the isolation of the altar as it was originally located at the rear of the choir and separated from the choir itself by a stone screen. In its own turn, the choir was surrounded on each side by choir-screens and was separated from the nave and the people by a high, solid, ornately sculptured rood-screen. All of these items have since almost completely disappeared, but their original installation is a clear reflection on the great separation that existed between people and altar.

Another concrete example of this trend is seen in the magnificent Cathedral of Chartres which also used to have a richly sculptured rood-screen which initiated a new High Gothic style. Erected about 1230 (destroyed in 1763), the screen consisted of a stage or loft that was more than sixty feet wide, supported by a solid partition on the choir side (with access through a central door) and in front upon an arcade of seven arches. This rood-screen was about twenty-five feet high. The only way we can gain a fairly accurate idea of its architecture is from old descriptions, pictures and fragments. The ornamental sculpture decorating the screen features scenes from the life of Christ as its principal theme. These sculptures are artistically valuable, and fragments have survived and are presently preserved in the crypt; however, the Louvre does possess one relief depicting the Evangelists.[26] The nativity of Christ is represented on another surviving fragment, and the style is close to that of the lintel reliefs of the Virgin door dating back to about the year 1210. It is a serene composition with the figure of the Virgin presenting a dignity and humanity that is extremely mature in its plasticity and naturalism. A remarkable likeness may be found in the Nativity fresco of the Arena Chapel in Padua painted one hundred years later by the great Italian master Giotto.[27]

A very interesting fact is that the cathedral canons had made a recommendation as late as 1514 that a stone screen be constructed around the chancel in order to provide an atmosphere of greater devotion and solemnity for the celebration of the sacred mysteries. Soon afterwards, the master Jean de Beauce began work on the project by initially masoning the two arcades between the roodloft and the high altar. At that time the high altar was situated in the middle of the chancel, and until 1520 the rood-screen did not stretch beyond this point. Now in the face of this new construction, the high altar, originally located between the second and third bays of the choir, was relocated to the rear of the chancel and the remainder of the screen was then completed.

> There are consequently two distinct constructions round the Cathedral choir and the High Altar: the more ancient one, which northward and southward, comprises the two first bays starting from the entrance, is more elegant and harmonious in design, than the other which was built, approximately, between 1520–1530, and fills up the spaces between the columns of the hemicycle and the two arcades preceding the apse. When Jean de Beauce died in 529, this encircling wall surrounded the choir on every side.[28]

Once again, in this cathedral, the main altar is isolated from the nave and the people by means of this high rood-screen and is located at the back of the enclosed chancel, the private sanctuary of the clergy, the holy of holies where the "sacred mysteries might be celebrated with more devotion and solemnity."[29]

Amiens Cathedral is another fine example of this trend for it also had a rood-screen of the Chartres type. However, as in the case of the original rood-screen at Chartres, it is unfortunately no longer in existence and is able to be known only from some old documents and drawings. Nonetheless, the present-day cathedral sufficiently evidences the effects of Eucharistic theology and popular piety upon the church building in the situation of the choir and high altar and its mitigated rood-screen which has now acquired the character of thin open-work. All of these elements, though somewhat changed over the years, are still able to give us a good concept of its former layout.[30]

As another illustration of this separation between altar and people, the Cathedral of Albi offers us a classic example. Seemingly untouched by time, this cathedral was built on the banks of the Tarn both as a house of worship and as an impregnable fortress. The first stone of this magnificently unified structure was laid by Bernard de Castanet on 15 August 1282. In about 1330–1340 the eastern half of the church was completed, and by 1390 the cathedral had been fairly well completed. Seen from within, the cathedral is simply an immense hall which had been constructed in an area of intense missionary activity and consequently had to be prepared both to defend itself and to preach the Word of God. The nave is uninterrupted by transepts or aisles and has chapels located between the internal abutment-piers.[31]

Despite its forboding and fortress-like appearance on the outside, within, this fortress-church possesses an atmosphere of calm and peacefulness, reflective of its charming patron Saint Cecilia. But for our purposes the most interesting aspect is the chancel in which the main altar is located and completely hidden from view of the nave behind one of the most remarkable rood-screens in existence. The rood-screen and the choir-screens were both erected about the year 1500 and are still in existence. The rood-screen divides the nearly three hundred foot length of the cathedral into two almost equal parts and is generally conceded to be unsurpassed anywhere. The statuary decorating this remarkable masterpiece "is surmounted by a magnificent frieze of lacy canopies and pinnacles."[32]

From this brief description, one can readily see how this entire choir and the altar within it is completely isolated from the nave and from the people, behind this impenetrable wall of rood-screen and choir-screen.

> At the very rear of the enclosed sanctuary, the high altar with its gradines and reredos is raised above the choir floor by several steps and is separated from the choir proper by a communion rail. The only view of the altar offered to the people in the nave is through the central door of the jube.[33]

All in all, I feel that this description offers us a very clear example of the spirit which governed the construction and the layout of this cathedral, a spirit which viewed the altar, sanctuary and choir as the private domain of the clergy. The beauty of Albi Cathedral is that it is today virtually untouched from its original construction and layout and therefore offers us a rare and intact view of the spirit of the times. This spirit not only resided in the Eucharistic theology and popular piety of the day, but it also took concrete form in the altar, its location and its decoration, as well as in the building which housed it and in the space which surrounded it.

In summary, the typical Gothic cathedral of the late Middle Ages seemed to embody certain basic elements. At the eastern end of the cathedral, its limbs were enclosed between the pillars by high stone screens which formed those areas reserved for the choir. At the western end of the choir was situated a double stone screen called the *pulpitum* or jube, which was surmounted by a loft upon which rested the nave rood, the choir organs, and a great lectern. The lower section was an arcade, and the only access to the choir was through the choir door located in the center of the arcade. On either side of the arcade were located the right and left nave altars. The original forms of the jubes of the cathedrals at Paris, Chartres, Strasbourg, and Amiens are no longer in existence and are only known from sketches taken before their destruction. As has previously been stated, several of the lovely sculptured panels which adorned the front of those at Chartres and also Bourges are still at least partially in existence. The high altar usually stood in the choir on the chord of the apse; to the rear, between the two central eastward columns, was the retro-altar, or altar of relics. A wonderfully detailed painting preserved at Arras entitled the "Mass of Saint Giles" is recognized as one of the best and most accurate illustrations of the original form and furnishings of such altars.[34]

> Six slender columns of bronze or silver stood, three on each side of the high altar, carrying rods to which were suspended curtains, and bearing figures of angels who held the instruments of the Passion. Above and behind the altar was a silver reredos, or "table" as it was called. The early silver reredos and the altar of Saint Denis are exquisitely delineated in this painting which was formerly attributed to the artist Jan Van Eyck, but which is now assigned to the Flemish Master of Saint Giles.[35]

Another exquisite example of such an altar is the high altar of Gerona Cathedral in Spain.[36]

At the Cathedral of Amiens a second stone screen rose up behind

the main altar like another pulpitum, with little winding stairs lead-
ing to a platform upon which were displayed the precious shrines
and other relics of the church. At the Sainte-Chapelle there was a
somewhat similar arrangement of great artistic beauty, but this platform with its open spiral steps was closer in resemblance to a baldachin. A *ciel* or tester was suspended above the high altar at Bourges;
rising higher yet was the choir-rood, surmounted with the gilded
and painted images of Saint Mary and Saint John. The tabernacle
housing the Blessed Sacrament was suspended from the tester while
to the left of the altar was a small chamber from which appointed
priests would be able to keep watch throughout the night over the
altar and its treasure. At Arras, visible over and beyond the high
altar was a large tabernacle for the preservation of relics supported
between the two eastern pillars and located directly above the relic
altar. A tall seven-branched candlestick stood guard before the high
altar.

> Across the choir ran a beam supporting lights, and to it was suspended
> the Lenten Veil, which divided the presbytery from the choir, on either
> side of which were stalls for the clergy and in the midst the eagle lectern.
> On feast days, fine tapestries were hung in the arches above the stalls.
> The bishop's throne, which earlier, in basilican arrangements, stood at
> the back of the apse, was later placed at the side of the altar.[37]

Thus, the French Gothic Cathedral of the late Middle Ages seems
to embody in its space, decoration and disposition, the apogee of
the various major trends of Eucharistic devotion and popular piety
to be found in the church of this era. As the art of the craftsman
grew, the more faithfully was he able to convey in stone, mortar,
space, lighting, precious metals and stones, stained glass and every-
thing else he could use, the living faith of his age.

Notes

[1] Louis Bouyer, *Liturgy and Architecture*, (Notre Dame: University of Notre
Dame Press, 1967), p. 79.

[2] Bernard Guillemain, *The Later Middle Ages*, trans. S. Taylor (New York:
Hawthorne Books, 1960), p. 29.

[3] J.G. Davies, *The Early Christian Church*, (Great Britain: Holt, Rinehart
and Winston, 1965), p. 152.

[4] R. Kevin Seasoltz, *The House of God*, (New York: Herder and Herder, 1963), p. 90.

[5] *Ibid.*, p. 92.

[6] *Ibid.*

[7] Davies, *op. cit.*, p. 269.

[8] F. van der Meer and Christine Mohrmann, *Atlas of the Early Christian World*, trans. and ed. Mary F. Hedlund and H.H. Rowley (London: Nelson, 1958), p. 135.

[9] Seasoltz, *op. cit.*, pp. 93–94.

[10] *Ibid.*, pp. 94–95.

[11] Johannes Wagner, "Liturgical Art and the Care of Souls," *The Assisi Papers*, (Collegeville: The Liturgical Press, 1957), p. 62.

[12] A.G. Hebert, *Liturgy and Society*, (New York: Faber and Faber, 1935), p. 75.

[13] Peter Hammond, *Liturgy and Architecture*, (New York: Columbia University Press, 1961), p. 18.

[14] Andre Bieler, *Architecture in Worship*, (Philadelphia: The Westminster Press, 1965), pp. 37–43.

[15] Hammond, *op. cit.*, pp. 18–19.

[16] Theodore Klauser, *A Short History of the Western Liturgy*, (London: Oxford University Press, 1969), pp. 100–101.

[17] Hammond, *op. cit.*, p. 19.

[18] Peter F. Anson, *Churches—Their Plan and Furnishing*, (Milwaukee: The Bruce Publishing Company, 1948), pp. 66–68.

[19] Hammond, *op. cit.*, pp. 19–20.

[20] *Ibid.*, p. 20.

[21] Hans Jantzen, *High Gothic*, trans. James Palmes (Great Britain: The Garden City Press, 1962), p. 47.

[22] Wilhelm Lubke, *Ecclesiastical Art in Germany During the Middle Ages*, trans. L.A. Wheatley (Edinburgh: Thomas C.Jack, 1870), p. 71.

[23] Allan Temko, *Notre-Dame of Paris* (New York: The Viking Press, 1959), p. 124.

[24] Marcel Aubert, *Gothic Cathedrals of France,* trans. Lionel and Miriam Kochan (London: Nicholas Kaye Limited, 1959), p. 52.

[25] *Ibid.*

[26] Jantzen, *op cit.,* pp. 62–63.

[27] George Henderson, *Chartres* (Great Britain: The Chaucer Press, 1968), p. 118.

[28] Rene Merlet, *The Cathedral of Chartres* (Paris: Henri Laurens, 1926), pp. 71–86.

[29] *Ibid.*

[30] Martin Hurlimann and Jean Bony, *French Cathedrals* (London: Thames and Hudson, 1967), p. 130.

[31] Aubert, *op. cit.,* pp. 101–102.

[32] *The Horizon Book Of Great Cathedrals,* ed. Jay Jacobs (New York: American Heritage Publishing Company, Inc., 1968), pp. 78–83.

[33] Aubert, *op. cit.,* pp. 424–425.

[34] Cyril E. Pocknee, *The Christian Altar* (London: A. R. Mowbray and Company Limited, 1963), p. 32.

[35] Martin Davies, *The Early Netherland School* (London: National Gallery Press, 1945), pl. 4681. The actual painting is presently located in the National Gallery, London.

[36] Pocknee, *op. cit.,* p. 23.

[37] W.R. Lethaby, *Medieval Art* (New York: Philosophical Library, 1950), p. 136.

Conclusion

The contention of this study has been that throughout the history of the Christian altar, in its location and decoration, it has been representative of various trends in Christian popular piety and Eucharistic devotion. The methodology of the research has been of historical nature, tracing the evolution of the altar in the primitive Church as table of the Lord to its position in the Middle Ages as grandiose and mysterious support and staging area for mysteries reserved to the witness of the clergy and from which the common man was excluded in the main.

Christian piety in the West had changed a great deal in the Middle Ages. Within the early Church the community of faith would gather around the table of the Lord for the joyful celebration of the Eucharistic Banquet in union with the Risen Lord. The community of faith of the Middle Ages, however, did not dare to draw near to the table of sacrifice. Instead, the faithful were relegated to a position from which they could merely bow to the altar from a distance and worship their Eucharistic Lord not through communion but through visual adoration. Originally rooted in a Resurrection faith, the Christian of the Middle Ages came to focus his devotional attention upon the passion and death of Christ, understanding the Mass principally—if not exclusively—as the bloody sacrifice of Christ. Derived from this mode of thought, the reconciliation of man to God was considered to be the product of their merits and penances rather than the gratuitous gift of grace bestowed through the Risen Lord's total victory over death.

Once again the altar resembles the seat of the sacrifices of the Old Testament with all their attendant ceremonial. Whereas at one time the priest faced the community across the altar, now he comes to the other side of the altar with his back to the people. The ancient pagan rites, so abhorrent to the early Christians, now seem to be influencing the mystery of Christianity in the realm of man's relationship to the deity. The conception of the Holy of Holies of the ancient Jerusalem Temple seems to be incorporated into the widening gulf between clergy and laity of the Middle Ages as altar and sanctuary become increasingly inaccessible to the people.

Where formerly the Church celebrated the liturgical mysteries as a true community united with its priest and each member with each other in mind and heart, now the community is transformed into a passive, anomalous crowd which merely watches the priest celebrate the liturgy on its behalf. The people become more and more dependent on the priest as they are no longer considered as indispensable partners. The process of clericalization caused the clergy to arrogate more and more of the liturgy to themselves, and they celebrated it in a more exclusive fashion within the protective enclave of the chancel. This area became the center of the Christian cult and the structure of the cathedral attests to this fact. The preeminent position of priest and altar are stressed in the cathedral layout. These magnificent cathedrals of the period are a living testimony of all these religious trends in their many different facets. The Eucharistic devotion and piety of the medieval man is faithfully translated and transcribed in these monuments to the faith of man.[1]

> As the Parthenon was the expression of a people inspired by the pricking desire for intellectual truth, so the churches of Christendom in the Gothic Age were the natural expressions of an age of faith. At Bourges, at Amiens, at Chartres, we watch the imaginations of disciplined artists steadily working out a vast, yet unified series of ideas which embody all the phases of religious emotion to be found in Christendom at the time of the Crusades. Forget the Catholic Church; forget the Crusades; and the minster and communal churches of Western Europe lose their deepest meaning. And not the walls, piers and vault alone, but all the arts associated with architecture must be borne in mind if the adventuring spirit is to learn the full meaning of a Gothic cathedral. Wall paintings, stained glass, and stone carvings were part of a whole which was greater than the building itself.[2]

In all aspects, the church building of the Middle Ages can be seen as a reflection of the on-going process of disintegration of the Church's worship and its effects on the faith-expression of the people. The Renaissance period essentially maintained this type of pattern. The Baroque period, however, made substantial changes such as the removal of the rood-screen and a genuine effort to unite the congregation once more in worship. This trend, nonetheless, did not restore a vital liturgy but merely fostered a type of service which was really nothing else than devotion to the Blessed Sacrament under the guise of liturgy.

Ever since the Baroque era, originality of church design had become almost non-existent. Architects were content to continue to merely copy the old Gothic and Baroque styles. The church building was no longer a true image of its own age but of an age gone by. The upheavals caused by the great World Wars surfaced a basic discontent with the lifeless repetition of the old styles of church architecture. A renewed interest in the liturgical life of the Church caused people to be much more concerned in this matter. All of these phenomena initiated some unusual and surprising developments.

> Architects ran, so to speak, ahead of developments in the liturgy; that is to say, they began to build churches which did not correspond to the actual liturgy of the day, but rather to a reformed kind of liturgy such as they hoped for in the future. They now began to construct the sacred area in such a way that the congregation celebrating the liturgy could once more feel themselves an entity, a unity or a family. It was intended that nothing should distract from the sacred action at the altar; hence the simplicity of the walls and ceiling, hence the disappearance of disturbing windows behind the altar; hence the sparing use of sculpture and painting. . . . [3]

Minus its gradines, retables, heavy painted panels, tabernacles, flowers, candelabra and lace, the altar looked once more like a table, despite efforts in the past to make it look like a monument. After its long development through history, the altar is finally returning to what it rightfully was at the beginning—a simple table. Now it is no longer unapproachable, a distant exhibit; but once again it has become the focal point for the worshipping community. The altar has returned as the table of the Lord; priest, altar and people are united once more.

Notes

[1] Andre Bieler, *Architecture in Worship* (Philadelphia: The Westminster Press, 1965) pp. 45–46.

[2] Ernest H. Short, *A History of Religious Architecture* (New York: The Macmillan Company, 1936), p. 15.

[3] Theodore Klauser, *A Short History of the Western Liturgy* (London: Oxford University Press, 1969) pp. 140–152.

Bibliography

Andrieu, Michel, *Les Ordines Romani du Haut Moyen Age*, 5 Vols. Louvain: Spicilegium Sacrum Lovanense, 1931–61. Vol. II.

Anson, Peter, *Churches: Their Plan and Furnishing*, Milwaukee: The Bruce Publishing Company, 1948.

Ante-Nicene Fathers, Vol. I, New York: Charles Scribners and Sons, 1926.

Aubert, Marcel, *Gothic Cathedrals of France*, translated by Lionel and Miriam Kochan, London: Nicholas Kaye Limited, 1959.

————, *The Art of the High Gothic Era*, New York: Crown Publishers, Inc., 1963.

Bieler, Andre, *Architecture in Worship*, Philadelphia: The Westminster Press, 1965.

Bishop, Edmund, *Liturgica Historica*, Oxford: The Clarendon Press, 1962.

Bouyer, Louis, *Liturgical Piety*, Notre Dame: University of Notre Dame Press, 1954.

————, *Liturgy and Architecture*, Notre Dame: University of Notre Dame Press, 1967.

————, *Eucharist*, Notre Dame: University of Notre Dame Press, 1968.

Braso, Gabriel M., *Liturgy and Spirituality*, translated by Leonard J. Doyle, Collegeville: The Liturgical Press, 1960.

Braun, Joseph, *Der christliche Altar in seiner geistlichen Entwicklung*, 2 Vols. Munich: Koch and Company, 1924.

Cabrol, F. and Leclercq, H., *Dictionnaire d'Archeologie Chretienne et de Liturgie*, 15 Vols. Paris, 1907–1953. Vols. I, III.

Comper, Ninina, *Of the Christian Altar—And the Buildings Which Contain It*, London: S.P.C.K., 1950.

Connolly, Hugh., (ed.), *Didascalia Apostolorum*, Oxford: The Clarendon Press, 1929.

Corpus Scriptorum Ecclesiasticorum Latinorum, edited by William Hartel. Vienna, 1866, et seqq, Vol. III.

Cross, F.L. (ed.), *The Oxford Dictionary of the Christian Church*, London: Oxford University Press, 1958.

Davies, J.G., *The Early Christian Church*, Great Britain: Holt, Rinehart and Winston, 1965.

Davies, Martin, *The Early Netherland School*, London: National Gallery Press, 1945.

Dix, Gregory, *A Detection of Aumbries*, London: Dacre Press, 1954.

Dolan, John P., *History of the Reformation*, New York: Désclee Company, 1965.

Dolger, Franz J., *Sol Salutis*, Munster: Aschendorff, 1925.

Duchesne, L., *Le Liber Pontificalis*, 2 Vols. Paris: E. De Boccard, 1955.

————, *Christian Worship*, London: S.P.C.K., 1904.

Eisenhofer, L. and Lechner, J., *The Liturgy of the Roman Rite*, translated by A.J. and E.F. Peeler. Edited by H.E. Winstone. New York: Herder and Herder, 1961.

Fortescue, Adrian, *The Mass—A Study of the Roman Liturgy*, New York: Longmans, Green and Company, 1937.

Franz, Adolf, *Die Messe in Deutschen Mittelalter*, Freiburg-im-Breisgau, 1902.

Funk, F.X. (ed.), *Didascalia et Constitutiones Apostolorum*, Paderborn: Libraria Ferdinandi Schoening, 1905.

Grossi-Gondi, Felice, *I Monumenti christiani*, Roma: Universita Gregoriana, 1923.

Guillemain, Bernard, *The Later Middle Ages*, translated by S. Taylor, New York: Hawthorne Books, 1960.

Hammond, Peter, *Liturgy and Architecture*, New York: Columbia University Press, 1961.

Herr, Friedrich, *The Medieval World*, translated by Janet Sondheimer, New York: The New American Library, 1962.

Hebert, A.G., *Liturgy and Society*, New York: Faber and Faber, 1935.

Henderson, George, *Chartres*, Great Britain: The Chaucer Press, 1968.

Hurlimann, Martin, and Bony, Jean, *French Cathedrals*, London: Thames and Hudson, 1967.

Jacobs, Jay (ed.), *The Horizon Book of Great Cathedrals*, New York: American Heritage Publishing Company, Inc., 1968.

Jantzen, Hans, *High Gothic*, translated by James Palmes. Great Britain: The Garden City Press, 1962.

Jungmann, Josef A., *The Mass of the Roman Rite*, 2 Vols., translated by Francis A. Brunner. New York: Benziger Brothers, Inc., 1951.

———, *The Early Liturgy*, Notre Dame: University of Notre Dame Press, 1959.

———, *Pastoral Liturgy*, New York: Herder and Herder, 1962.

———, *The Good News Yesterday and Today*, translated and edited by William A. Huesman, New York: W.H. Sadlier, Inc., 1962.

———, *Public Worship*, Collegeville: The Liturgical Press, 1957.

———, *The Place of Christ in Liturgical Prayer*, translated by A. Peeler, New York: Alba House, 1965.

Kidd, B.J., *The Later Medieval Doctrine of the Eucharistic Sacrifice*, London: Society for Promoting Christian Knowledge, 1958.

King, Archdale A., *Eucharistic Reservation in the Western Church*, New York: Sheed and Ward, 1965.

Klauser, Theodore, *A Short History of the Western Liturgy*, London: Oxford University Press, 1969.

Lethaby, W.R., *Medieval Art*, New York: Philosophical Library, 1950.

Liesting, G.T.H., *The Sacrament of the Liturgy*, New York: Newman Press, 1968.

Lubke, Wilhelm, *Ecclesiastical Art in Germany During the Middle Ages*, translated by L.A. Wheatley. Edinburgh: Thomas C. Jack, 1870.

Maffei, E., *La Reservation Eucharistique jusqu'à la Renaissance*, Bruxelles: Eds Vromant S.A., 1942.

Male, Emile, *La Cathedral d'Albi*, Paul Hartman, ed. Dijon: A. Daranthiere, 1950.

Mansi, J.D. (ed.), *Sacrorum Conciliorum nova et amplissima Collectio*, 31 Vols. Florence, 1759–98, Vol. VIII.

Meer, F. van der, and Mohrmann, Christine, *Atlas of the Early Christian World*, translated and edited by Mary F. Hedlund and H.H. Rowley. London: Thomas Nelson and Sons Limited, 1958.

Merlet, Rene, *The Cathedral of Chartres*, Paris: Henri Laurens, 1926.

Migne, J.P., (ed.), *Patrologia Graeca*, 166 Vols. Paris, 1844, et seqq. Vols. III, X, XXXXVI.

Migne, J.P. (ed.), *Patrologia Latina*, 217 Vols. 1844, et seqq. Vols. XXXIII, XXXV, LXI.

Miller, John H., *Fundamentals of the Liturgy*, Notre Dame: Fides Publishers Inc., 1962.

Minchin, Basil, *The Celebration of the Eucharist—Facing the People*, London: Darton, Longman and Todd, Ltd., 1961.

———, *Outward And Visible*, London: Darton, Longman and Todd, Ltd. 1961.

Neunheuser, B., *L'Eucharistie—Au Moyen Age et à l'Epoque Modern*, translated by A. Liefooghe, Paris: Les Editions du Cerf, 1966.

O'Shea, William J., *The Worship of the Church*, Maryland: The Newman Press, 1958.

O'Connell, J.B., *Church Building and Furnishing*, Notre Dame: University of Notre Dame Press, 1955.

Palanque, Jean-Remy, *The Dawn of the Middle Ages*, translated by Dom Finbarr Murphy. New York: Hawthorne Books, 1960.

Pirenne, Henri, *Medieval Cities*, translated by Frank D. Halsey. New York: Doubleday and Company, Inc., 1956.

Pocknee, Cyril E., *The Christian Altar*, London: A.R. Mowbray and Company Limited, 1963.

Quasten, Johannes, *Patrology*, 3 Vols. Utrecht: Spectrum Publishers, 1966.

———, *Monumenta eucharistica et liturgica vetustissima, Florilegium Patristicum*, 7 Vols. Bonn: Peter Hansetein, 1935

Seasoltz, Kevin R., *The House of God*, New York: Herder and Herder, 1963.

Sheppard, Lancelot (ed.), *True Worship*, Baltimore: The Helicon Press, 1963.

Short, Ernest H., *A History of Religious Architecture*, New York: The Macmillan Company, 1936.

Temko, Allan, *Notre-Dame of Paris*, New York: The Viking Press, 1959.

Verheul, A., *Introduction to the Liturgy*, Collegeville: The Liturgical Press, 1968.

Webb, Geoffrey, *The Liturgical Altar*, London: Washbourne and Bogan, Ltd., 1933.

Westow, Theodore, *The Variety of Catholic Attitudes*, New York: Herder and Herder, 1963.

Wilson, H.A. (ed.), *The Gelasian Sacramentary*, Oxford, 1894.

Articles

Andrieu, Michel, "Note sur une ancienne redaction de l'Ordo Romanus Primus," *Revue des Sciences Religieuses*, I (1921).

Bishop, Edmund, "On the History of the Christian Altar," *Downside Review*, July 1905, pp. 154–182.

Boulet, Noele-Maurice, "L'autel dans l'antiquité chretienne," *La Maison-Dieu*, XXIX (1952), p. 45.

Gelin, Albert, "L'autel dans l'Ancien Testament," *La Maison-Dieu*, XXIV (1952), pp. 9–17.

Jungmann, Josef A., "The New Altar," *Liturgical Arts*, XXXVII (February, 1969), p. 37.

Leclercq, Henri, "Le mystere de l'autel," *La Maison-Dieu*, XXIX (1952), pp. 60–70.

———, "Orientation," *Dictionnaire d'archéologie chrétienne et de liturgie*, XII (1936), pp. 2665–2666.

———, "Autel," *Dictionnaire d'archéologie chrétienne et de liturgie*, VI (1924), pp. 3158–3161.

Miller, John H., "Altar Facing The People, Fact or Fable?" *Worship*, XXXIII (January, 1959) pp. 85–86.

Rousseau, Oliver, "Le Christ et l'autel: note sur la tradition patristique," *La Maison-Dieu*, XXIX (1952), pp. 32–39.

Schmitt, Joseph, "Petra autem erat Christus," *La Maison-Dieu*, XXIV (1952), pp. 18–31.

Wagner, Johannes, "Liturgical Art and the Care of Souls," *The Assisi Papers*, (Collegeville: The Liturgical Press, 1957), pp. 57–73.

Index